Pitney Bowes

Mail it!

*High-Impact Business Mail
From Design to Delivery*

A Pitney Bowes *Best Practices* Guide

Alice Powers McElhone and Edward B. Butler

MAIL IT!

PUBLISHED BY
Benchmark Publications Inc.
76 Elm Street - P.O. Box 1594
New Canaan, Connecticut 06840-1594

Mail It! High-Impact Business Mail from Design to Delivery
by Alice Powers McElhone and Edward B. Butler
Book design and illustrations by John Williams

Library of Congress Catalog Card Number: 95-79158
ISBN 0-09647121-0-5

Printed and bound in the United States of America.

Trademark Information

CAT and Caterpillar are registered trademarks of Caterpillar Corporation

CentraLink is a service mark of SNET CentraLink

Postage-by-Phone is a registered trademark of Pitney Bowes, Inc.

Mail It!, SmartMailer, Postal Coding for SmartMailer, Dupe Detect for SmartMailer and Presort for SmartMailer are trademarks of Pitney Bowes, Inc.

Aldus PageMaker is a registered trademark of Adobe Systems Inc.

Conquest for Windows and Atlas GIS for Windows are registered trademarks of Strategic Mapping Inc.

DirectNET is a service mark of Pitney Bowes, Inc.

Excel, Foxpro, Microsoft, MS-DOS, and Windows are registered trademarks of Microsoft Corporation

FileMaker and MacWrite are registered trademarks of Claris Corporation

Macintosh, MacOS and Mac are registered trademarks of Apple Computer

MTST, Electromatic and System 6 are trademarks of International Business Machines Inc.

PaperDirect is a registered trademark of Paper Direct, Inc.

United States Postal Service and USPS are trademarks of the United States Postal Service

WordPerfect and ExpressDoc are registered trademarks of WordPerfect Corporation

Xerox and the XEROX logo are registered trademarks of Xerox Corporation

ZIP Code, ZIP+4, First-Class, POSTNET and DPBC are registered trademarks of the United States Postal Service

All other product and trade names mentioned in this book are the property of their respective owners.

Special thanks to...

Pitney Bowes, Inc.

...and to Microsoft Corporation for sharing some useful tools and technical support, and for permission to use Microsoft Word for Windows 6.0 for all of the word processing screens in this book.

...and thanks to all the *Mail It!* design experts at:

Caterpillar Corporation

General Electric Company

Paper Direct, Inc.

Pitney Bowes, Inc.

SNET

United States Postal Service

USPS Stamford Business Center

Xerox Corporation

Contents

Illustrations

Mail It!

High-Impact Business Mail from Design to Delivery

This book is about designing and producing better looking business mail and getting it to the right destination on time. It's written for people who want to know just enough about design, technology and postal standards to get their mail out the door, looking great.

A companion book published in 1992, *How to Grow Your Business Using the Mail*, gives excellent advice and information on targeting your market and using direct mail to reach it. *Mail It!™ High-Impact Business Mail* follows up by helping you prepare well-designed, technically correct documents to carry your message to your customers.

Businesses of all sizes and kinds have invested heavily in personal computers (PCs), yet many of these organizations don't come close to realizing the full potential of their investment. And all too few of us take advantage of the nation's new automated postal system.

Mail It! shows you how to apply today's technology to design, produce and deliver your business communications better, faster and more economically.

Taking the Awe out of Automation

PCs have been familiar features on the business landscape for almost two decades, yet many people either still resist using them or use only the most basic features. Part of the problem is that although computer hardware is becoming much simpler and faster, software is becoming more complex.

It's been said that 80% of all personal computer users understand and use no more than 20% of their everyday software programs' functions. That isn't surprising. As this book goes to press, the current editions of the two most popular word processing programs are accompanied by 829- and 986-page manuals respectively. (In one, the Index alone is 44 pages of very small type.) That covers a lot of functions, some of which are understood and used by only a tiny fraction of the total PC community.

This book explains the concepts common to all PCs and software programs— fundamental information that's hard to find in a software manual.

As it has changed the office, automation has also changed the way the postal system works. The 882-page USPS *Domestic Mail Manual 48* offers so many mailing options you need a guide to the manual (one is provided). Guessing wrong can be costly. *Mail It!* gives you clear guidelines for addressing your business mail correctly and keeping your mailing list up to date.

Mail It! won't make you an expert in word processing, desktop marketing, list management or the workings of the nation's postal system. It *will* show you the basics you need right now.

About this Book

Mail It! is organized in four chapters with a look-up reference.

■ DESIGN: simple guidelines for designing more effective business communications, with models from the experts. This is not a comprehensive design tutorial; these easy tips will point you in the right direction for improving your organization's professional image.

■ DESKTOP MARKETING: pointers for developing a beginner's marketing kit; more expert advice and examples from some well-known corporations.

■ PRODUCTION: concepts about using your PC as a business mail production machine and producing P.C. (Postally Correct) business mail.

■ DELIVERY: accurate information on how you can meet the U.S. Postal Service halfway to give your mail the swiftest, surest route through the system.

■ REFERENCE: a brief refresher course on personal computing; an introduction to list management software, and useful facts related to the major topics.

About the Screens

Many of the concepts discussed in *Mail It!* are common to other software programs. For simplicity, they are illustrated with replicas of screens from these programs, with the generous permission of their publishers:

AddressMate for Windows
© 1994 AddressMate Software
Co-Star Corporation

Aldus PageMaker
© 1993 Aldus Corporation, © 1995 Adobe Corporation

Atlas GIS for Windows
© 1994, 1995 Strategic Mapping, Inc.

FileMaker Pro
© 1990, 1992 Claris Corporation

Microsoft Excel
© 1993 Microsoft Corporation

Microsoft Word for Windows
© 1993, 1994 Microsoft Corporation

SmartMailer: Postal Coding, Dupe Detect and Presort
© 1994, 1995 Pitney Bowes, Inc.

Design

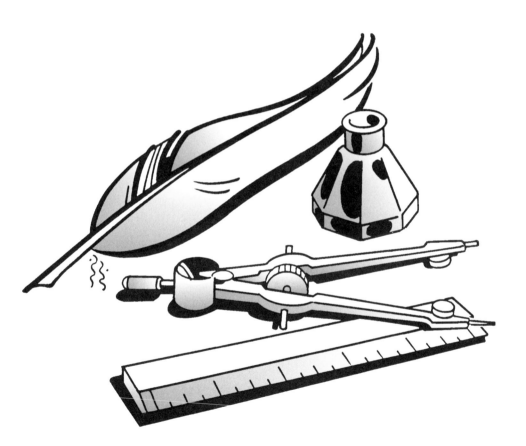

Design

Have you noticed how quickly your in-basket fills up these days? (So much for the paperless office.) In fact, in the first ten years of desktop computing, the demand for office paper *increased* 7.4 percent, or three times as fast as the Gross Domestic Product (GDP) during that period. Imagine what it must be today.

You've heard this before: Every envelope in that in-basket is competing for your attention. Which one will you open first? Your outbound correspondence faces the same fierce competition. To stay in the game, you have to know the fundamentals of effective business communications: formal letters, promotional letters, postcards, direct marketing pieces and more. Even if you don't do your own correspondence, you should know what it takes to get it read.

This chapter is all about:

- Your Professional Image
- Writing Letter Perfect documents

Professional Image

Even today's warp-speed communications can't replace a well-crafted, image-conscious personal letter to a customer…or a handsome newsletter that keeps your audience informed…or even a professionally produced, crisp and readable invoice. Every time you correspond with a customer, you're saying either "We're indifferent to your reaction to this," or "We know what we're doing and we value your opinion of us."

What are your business communications trying to do? Inform, convince, persuade? You may think if your message is genuine it doesn't matter what it looks like, but that is decidedly not the case. The use of modern tools like typography, graphics and color "makes a direct, measurable impact on the readability, memorability and persuasion power of your documents."[1] Look again at the mail in your in-basket—more color, better design, greater impact. Isn't it time your company got up to speed?

The Big Picture

Take a wide-angle picture of the mail your company sends today. Is it distinctive? uniform? Does it say something definitive about your company? A fledgling enterprise can look just as professional as the giants by learning from the well-tested wisdom of their designers.

---

1 from *Great Originals,* a symposium on document design,
  © 1986 Xerox Corporation

You may be just starting out or changing your company's image. In either case, you can benefit from this quick look at a few basic design elements and how they are used by well-known corporations.

The logo is a central element in the corporate statement. You can recognize the Westinghouse W and the CBS Eye without another single word. In the marketplace, that's money in the bank. Companies take great care to preserve the integrity of the logo: It is always positioned precisely, printed in the approved coloring and used only on official publications or structures. A logo doesn't have to be elaborate or expensive, but once you choose it, always use it the same way to establish your own identity.

If you aren't ready to develop a corporate logo, your corporate signature can serve to single you out from the crowd.

The corporate signature can be a combination of the company name, with or without the logo, with additional graphics or text such as a stripe or a slogan or both. It's also referred to as the company's graphic signature. It can be as simple as the typographic treatment of your company name or as elaborate as a graphic representation of the company nickname. Whatever components you choose, the typography, color, position and usage of the signature should be defined and followed consistently. (Design at least two versions: one for black and white publications and one for color work.)

Corporate grids are used by many identity-conscious companies to prescribe layouts for their publications with positioning for logos and signatures—from a letter to a catalog to the signage on a company building. The underlying structure helps designers take advantage of the established recognition factors. Grids shouldn't be complicated. The challenge is to provide a solid structure that still allows a measure of freedom and creativity.

Don't be afraid to make a bold statement with your company identity. As your business grows and changes, your logo and signature can change as well, as long as you plan your transformations deliberately.

Expert Testimony

Xerox Corporation, one of the pioneers in document design, has a highly developed system of publishing standards. As early as 1980, a Xerox "Document Creation Center" staff typed every business letter on word processors, strictly matching a printed overlay. The text lined up smartly at the same left margin as the letterhead legend, at a carefully calculated distance from the top (adjusted for length), as precise as a military blueprint.

For years, you could spot Xerox publications and advertisements immediately because of a distinctive broad band of color across the top, a unifying device used until very recently. A hidden structure organized the elements on the page. The result was a clean, sure-footed look that was instantly recognizable.

Nothing is forever. As products, markets and technologies evolve over the years, so does a company's graphic signature. The next page shows an example of how a business maintains its identity as it responds to advancing technologies.

Evolution of a Corporate Identity—Logos courtesy of Xerox Corporation

Smart communicators put a lot of effort into the recognition factor. Companies and institutions publish standards and guidelines for communications people to follow. Standards ensure uniformity and the correct use of the organization's identity factors: the corporate logo, the corporate signature, the corporate colors and even the corporate typeface.

Corporate ID guidelines can be formidable. General Electric's two-volume *GE Identity Program* weighs in at 15 pounds and keeps firm control over the troops of designers who prepare its publications. (In tune with the times, GE now produces these volumes on CD-ROM.)

Notice the narrow columns in the GE grid for product brochures on the next few pages. The columns can be combined into wider blocks for cover illustrations and inner text and graphics.

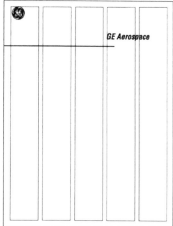

Use a grid. A grid is an underlying structure used to organize graphic and typographic elements in a layout. By vertically and horizontally aligning these elements at common points on the grid, an orderly appearance is created which communicates a sense of planning, discipline and professionalism.
• Use a single grid for the covers and inside spreads of a brochure or a series of related brochures.
• Use a grid tailored to your needs. Three-column, four-column, five-column, and six-column grids–any of these and others may be used in print applications; no particular grid is recommended.

Use a Graphic Signature
• at the top of the front cover or outside panel and
• on the back cover or panel, with an address block, if desired.
• Note: A Graphic Signature is *required* in all print applications.
• For guidelines on the construction of Graphic Signatures, see Volume I, Section 5.

Building the grid—Courtesy of General Electric Company

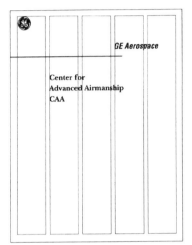 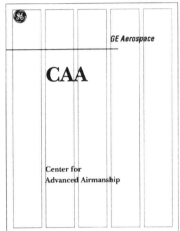

Use a basic layout established by the selected grid and the placement of the Graphic Signature on the grid as shown in the examples.

• Use an asymmetrical layout with generous clear space. One method of creating this appearance is to emphasize the Signature Monogram by keeping the left column of the grid clear.

• Align other graphic and typographic elements on the grid.

Prioritize information.

• **Emphasize information of primary importance** by either:
- using it in the typography of the Graphic Signature, or
- placing it outside the signature, using a large size and/or a heavy weight of Program Typography, and accenting it with color.

• **De-emphasize information of secondary importance** by placing it outside the signature, using a small size and/or a light weight of Program Typography, and subduing it with color.

continued

Grids provide structure to a family of publications.

—Courtesy of General Electric Company

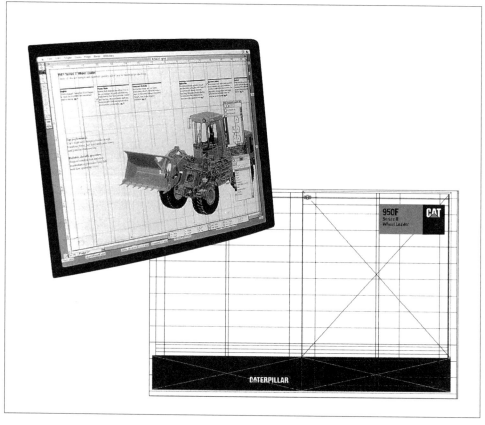

The architecture of a "specalog"—Courtesy of Caterpillar Inc.

Caterpillar's flexible guidelines vary for each of their audiences: employees, customers, dealers, shareholders and the public. This electronic template for a spec sheet/catalog grid speeds the work of their designers.

There is method behind this obsessive attention to detail. Well-documented studies, such as a now-classic work by the Wharton Center for Applied Research, have shown that carefully structured business documents are easier to read, easier to understand, easier to remember, and produce more favorable results.

These are certainly valid reasons to pay attention to white space, choice of type, use of graphics and other matters that once belonged only to the world of graphic design. Now that these basic design elements can be produced easily on a personal computer, you can lift your correspondence out of the *ho-hum* pile to the *immediate attention* stack.

Imitate!

You say your company isn't Xerox, GE or Caterpillar and maybe a designer would strain your budget right now. Well, do as the designers do: Borrow ideas and try them out on your PC before you commit to printing.

Most feature-rich word processing packages include an assortment of templates—preformatted layouts that take the guesswork out of page design. Try them all, but don't stop there. Customize the templates that work for you to give your organization its distinctive identity. You don't want your correspondence to look like everyone else's—just better.

Another way to formulate your company's look is to collect the best of each kind of business mail that comes your way. Experiment with the layout grid from one, a type family from another and a color scheme from third, and you'll begin to develop your own look.

A good place to start is with your corporate letterhead. All your letters should be set up to complement the letterhead, but you have to do a lot more than line up your margins. You need today's tools to produce a polished, professional look.

Later in this chapter, you'll read about the content of your documents. These next ideas concern the overall appearance.

Design 101

It's said that we accept new information through all of our five senses: taste (1%), touch (1.5%), smell (3.5%), hearing (11%) and sight (a whopping 83%). That's why it's important to pay attention to the design of your business communications. "Documents don't say, they show. Well-designed documents persuade readers to absorb the thoughts on the paper through their eyes."[2]

Many cognitive psychologists, who deal with the matters of judgment and awareness, agree that the way a page looks has a strong influence on the reader's ability to understand, remember and recall information. Recall and understanding are requisites for taking action.

No single authority has all the answers to such a subjective matter as design, so like the rest of us, you'll have to learn to rely on your own eye. A few simple guidelines will show you what to look for. (If some of the terms aren't familiar, check the Glossary.) Rules are made to be broken, but unless you're very sure of yourself, keep these tips in mind:

- The eye reads text from left to right, graphics from upper left to lower right. Decide which element—copy or picture—is most important for the page and put that element in the dominant quarter.

- In a long document, text should be no wider on the page than about 4½ or 5 inches to avoid tiring the reader's eyes.

- Columns of text are ideally at least 2¼ inches wide to keep the reader from having to scan too many lines to get the meaning of a sentence.

- Too much information on one page is confusing. Use one significant picture, or maybe two, on a standard size page that also presents important text. If there are more pictures than text, consider a whole page devoted to graphics with the text on a facing page.

2 *Great Originals Seminar,* Xerox Corporation

- Left and right margins can be equal, but top and bottom margins should not. (When typewriters were common, the rule was more space at the bottom, but now the placement of the white space is dictated by the content or logotype design.)

- For longer works like a company brochure, look at facing pages when you lay it out. Visual elements like margins, rules and text should line up across the spread.

- Treat white space as a positive design element. Look at the entire page as you design, all the way out to all four edges.

> ***Take the Long View.*** *Hold the page far enough away so you can't read the text. Check for balance, distribution of white space and especially for distracting "rivers"— patterns of white space running through solid text blocks.*

- Folios (page numbers) are easiest to find at the outside corners of the page, in the top or bottom margin.

- Avoid too many levels of indentation. The zigzag effect destroys the unity of your design.

- Think of headings and the following copy as one unit. Keep headings and subheadings close to the copy they control. Add white space above the heading to set off the new unit.

- Place numbers and bullets close to the text they set off.

- In a formal business document, headings should be close enough in size to the body copy to give a feeling of unity, but distinct enough to make the structure clear.

For example, if the body text of your document is 12-point type, keep your headings and subheadings in the 14- to 24-point range. A 48-point heading overpowers 12-point copy. (Direct marketing and advertising copy veterans bend these rules frequently, but maybe you should wait until you're sure of yourself with typography.)

Use variations of roman (upright) and italic (slanted), bold and regular fonts, or varying weights of rules (lines) to show the hierarchy of your headings.

Now let's look at the technology that makes all this easy.

21st Century Editing

Of all the computer programs for the PC, the word processor (WP) is probably the most widely used. The primary advantages of an electronic word processor over an "acoustic" system are image, speed and productivity.

Word processors can do this to your documents:

- Move, copy, insert and delete a character, a word, a sentence, a paragraph or a picture.

- Check your spelling.

- Apply a special format to a word, sentence, paragraph, page or document automatically.

- Replace a word or phrase universally.

- Present your words in a variety of font sizes and styles.

(If your word processor can't do this much, it's a line editor, more at home on a mainframe than a PC.)

This section introduces you to the single most important feature of word processing that makes all the rest of it work—*word wrap.* Then you'll learn about the powerful features that affect the overall document, and finally, we'll look at typography in more depth.

> *A **Working Relationship.** With most software virtually any special function is an interaction between you and the system. It goes like this:*
>
> *Define:*   *Highlight the work to be acted on.*
>
> *Command:* *Select the appropriate command or option.*
>
> *Accept:*   *Use Enter or OK to approve the change and exit the function.*
>
> *The order of these actions may vary, but all three are needed.*

Word Wrap

Word wrap is the revolutionary invention at the heart of word processing editing capabilities. Word wrap has canceled out the carriage return. On a word processor, you just type until you want to start a new paragraph. The system automatically returns to the left margin as each line fills up.

Insert and Delete: Remember inserting a word in a pre-electronic letter? Deleting was fun, too—all those unsightly gaps or layers of white paint. Some of us even remember slicing type and sliding it over to make room for a word or to cover up a hole. Word wrap changed all that. Add the missing words and the text opens up to make room. Remove the offending words and the text flows back over the gap.

Copy and Move used to be done with scissors and tape. Now you use a special key or command to select the text to work with, complete the action and let word wrap do the rest. When you make changes, the elastic lines rewrap. No retyping!

Global Changes

All but the puniest text editor can make sweeping changes that affect a whole document without human intervention.

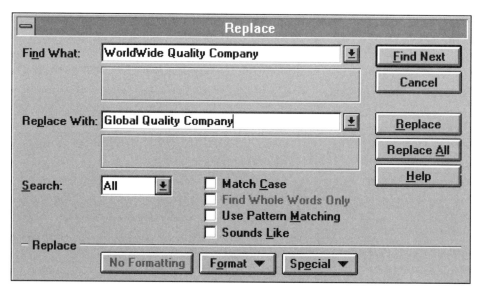

Replace *saves the day*

Microsoft Word for Windows 6.0 dialog box—Courtesy of Microsoft Corporation

Search and Replace is very nearly a religious experience to every new convert to WP. (Your word processor may call it something like Find and

Replace, or just Replace.) Say, to your horror, you've misspelled the prospect's name throughout a ten-page proposal. On your word processor, enter the wrong word in the designated place, then enter the right word. Press the button (or key) and watch the show.

Spelling and Grammar Checking are justifiably revered WP features. People with great ideas and a shaky recall of sixth grade English class write with confidence with the help of the built-in spelling checker. It isn't foolproof, of course. It can't tell the difference between *there* and *their,* but it knows *ther* is wrong. A grammar checker might catch *Put it their* for *Put it there.*

Page Formatting

Here are a few tricks that will bring your page design or document structure to life:

Text Alignment: Do you need an extra-formal look? A word processor can line up the text with straight left and right margins (right-justified). However, for most purposes, rag right (a ragged right margin) is a good choice. If you choose justified type, you should know something about hyphenation and character spacing or your page could develop an ungainly look as the system s t r e t c h e s a loose line to meet the requirement of a straight right margin. Rag right is reported to be easier to read, too.

Widows and Orphans are dead giveaways of a novice at work. A widow is a single line at the beginning of a paragraph left stranded at the bottom of a column or page. An orphan is the last line of a paragraph that spills over onto the next column or page. The saddest widow or orphan of all is the single word or even a part of a hyphenated word that is stranded. Rescue

your widows and orphans if you want to look like a pro. In most word processors, you can force a line end to push more text to the next column or page with a key combination such as SHIFT | ENTER.

> **Forced Endings.** *To keep your document flexible until you're ready to print, don't force line endings until the very last edit or you'll lose the advantage of word wrap.*

Margins, Tabs and Indents: Three dreaded tasks for typists are setting margins and tabs, and typing indents, hanging and otherwise. You can do these things more-or-less automatically on most electronic typewriters, but it isn't easy. A word processor offers a visual reference on the screen (usually a tab or format ruler or a miniature sample) to help you set up the page.

WP programs have preset (default) regular tabs every five spaces or so. Maybe you've been using these settings because you thought they were recommended. In fact, this setting is almost never quite right for anything. It's a hangover from the days when everything was typed in Courier 10-pitch (10 characters to the inch), 80 characters to the line. In contrast, 10-point Times Roman (not 10-pitch) yields more like 18 characters to an inch. That's why the default indents and tabs look so awkward with some type sizes. You can reset the spacing of indents and tabs to suit each of the typestyles and sizes you use.

Left-aligned tabs (regular tabs), right-aligned tabs, center tabs and decimal tabs are more text design tools available now. The decimal tab has changed statistical typing forever. On a conventional typewriter, decimal numbers such as dollar amounts have to be lined up manually.

September 1, 1996¶
¶
¶
Mr. Vincent Van Gogh¶
Hollywood Arts Distributing¶
5555 Hollywood Boulevard¶
P.O. Box 5555¶
Los Angeles, CA 90029-5555¶
¶
¶
Dear Vince:¶
¶
Here are the results of the sales competition. Although your
group did not win the trip to Hawaii, you made a very good
showing.¶
¶

→	Posters	→	Videos	→	Collectibles¶
East Coast →	25,543.50	→	35,500.25	→	32,400.25¶
West Coast →	24,450.25	→	33,300.33	→	24,230.60¶
MidWest →	9,689.50	→	6,500.00	→	9,689.50¶
Mountain States →9,000.00	→	15,000.00	→	8976.40¶

¶
  → Keep up the good work!¶
¶
Sincerely,¶
¶
¶
¶
Charlie David¶
President¶

Try that on your typewriter!

With a word processing program (and some electronic typewriters), you tab to a decimal tab stop and type the number. The system aligns the numbers to the left and right of the period.

On most popular word processors, an indent is easily set either on the format ruler or with a special tab or key combination. You just move a special marker to set an indent margin on the ruler.

> ### *Hanging Indents.*
>
> 1. *Use hanging indents*   ■ *Hanging indents work*
>   *for steps.*   *for bullets, too.*

Hanging indents are special paragraph treatments worth knowing how to do. Use them for steps and bullets, but be sure you know the difference.

Steps are for sequential events or instructions:

1. I came.

2. I saw.

3. I conquered.

Bullets are for important information.

All Gaul is divided into three parts:

■ Part I – Home of the Belgae

■ Part II – Home of the Aquitani

■ Part III – Home of the Celts

Notice how much closer the text is to these numerals and bullets.

Once you've determined the best look for your corporate correspondence, make sure everyone in the office follows the standard format. Set the defaults on the systems to accommodate your preprinted letterhead. It's an inexpensive, effective way to start building your own recognition factor.

> ***Learn to Format; Rule the World.*** *If you learn no other feature on your word processor, learn to set margins, tabs and indents.*

Organizing Principles

Some page formatting operations serve to organize a document to make it easier for you to work with and easier for your audience to read.

Running Text: A header or footer is running text that appears in the margin at the top or bottom of every page. It serves as a visual organizer for your reader. With a word processing program, you type the text once and it's automatically repeated on each page—or every odd or even page, if you choose. A page number in a header or footer is incremented automatically, and if you add a page, the system renumbers the document for you.

A toolbar for headers and footers

Outlines: Many WP programs offer different views of the page, the most useful being outline form. Use this function to organize your ideas and to make sure your work-in-progress adheres to the structure you've defined.

Tables: Numeric or textual data can be organized in a row/column format to make statistical or comparative material more accessible to the reader.

"Tables are clearly the way to show exact numerical values.... Tables are preferable to graphics for many small data sets." [3]

...and yet we continue to make people read comparative data in prose because tables are supposed to be hard to make. A veteran writer with more than ten years of word processing says, *"I don't do windows and I don't do tables."*

Tables offer a distinct advantage over tab settings for tabular data. The text in each cell of a table can be word-wrapped independent of the other cells (the spaces bounded by the intersections of rows and columns) or columns. Even better, you can add, delete, copy and move columns until you get your table just right. Try *that* with data or text lined up on tabs.

Don't be afraid of tables. You can always Undo or Delete and start over. (Check the Edit menu for these commands.) At least one word processor has two very useful self-explanatory commands: Convert Text to Table and Convert Table to Text. Now that's the easy way. Try it—what do you have to lose? Just *define, command* and *accept.*

3 *The Visual Display of Quantitative Information,*
Edward R. Lufte, © 1983 Graphics Press

Your WP program may offer several templates for tables. Choose a template and fill in the cells.

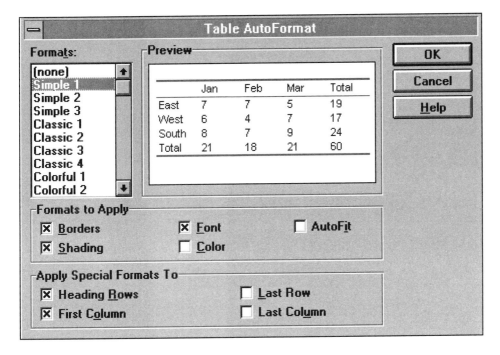

Templates make tables easy.

Here are generic steps for creating a table from scratch, without a template:

1. In an open document, choose the menu option or key combination for inserting a table.

   A prompt or dialog box pops up.

2. Specify the number of columns and rows.

3. Find and use the function for defining the character and number formats for the data that goes in the cells.

(For example, if it's a column of numbers, do you want a dollar sign and two zeros? Check the Format or Edit menu for these options.)

4. Enter the data, tabbing between cells.

5. Save your document; the table is saved with it.

When you've learned this much, be brave. Read the user guide and learn more.

Graphs and Graphics: Data too complex for a table can be added to your business correspondence as a graph from your spreadsheet program. Here's how:

1. Open a new worksheet.

2. Enter the labels and numbers.

3. Highlight the part to be plotted as a graph. (Remember, *define, command* and *accept.*)

Select one or more columns for a pie chart, and at least two columns for other charts so there's something to compare.

	A	B	C	D	E	F
1			Quantity	Price	Total	
2	Ceiling white		90 qts	$25.00	$2,250.00	
3	Blue gouache		20 gals	$45.00	$900.00	
4	Rose oil		30.5 gals	$45.00	$1,372.50	
5	Gold leaf		10 gals	$98.50	$985.00	
6						
7	Grand total				$5,507.50	

Microsoft Excel — ANGELO1.XLS

File Edit View Insert Format Tools Data Window Help

Arial   10

B22

A spreadsheet program can work with your word processor.

Microsoft Excel—Courtesy of Microsoft Corporation

4. Choose the graphing command (usually a menu pick or icon).

5. Select the graph type.

6. Choose any other options offered, such as colors, special effects, legends and titling.

7. Save the graph as a separate sheet or document.

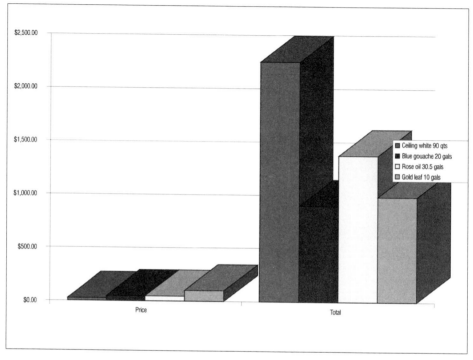

The data become a picture...

Now you can pop the graph right into your letter. (This method works for the Macintosh and for Windows. Other operating systems may take a few more steps.)

1. Copy the chart.

2. Open the letter.

3. Set the cursor where the graph belongs.

   Paste the chart into the letter. (Check the Edit menu for the Paste command.)

   When the graph appears in the document on your screen, you can move it or size it.

4. Save the finished product.

> **Task Switching.** *Under the Windows and Mac operating systems, you don't have to exit the spreadsheet to go to the word processor. Look up Control Menu or Task List in the Windows User Guide, or Application Menu in the Macintosh Reference. Switching between open applications can save you from hours of wasted motion.*

For something a little less ambitious, most popular word processing packages include clip art that can be popped right into an informal document to add punch. Certain other picture formats can be placed in other documents, too. A good painting or drawing software program can save artwork in several file formats: .PCX, .TIF (or TIFF) graphic file formats are most widely accepted by word processing and page composition programs on all platforms.

September 1, 1996

Mr. Michael Angelo
Vice President, Facilities
Sistine Systems, Inc.
P.O. Box 1110
Rome, NY 13440-1110

Re: Summary of products purchased

Dear Mr. Angelo:

It was truly a shame about the fire. We are willing to comply with your somewhat unusual request for a summary of your purchases by product. I will call you personally on Friday to work out a schedule of payment. This graph gives you a good snapshot of your current situation:

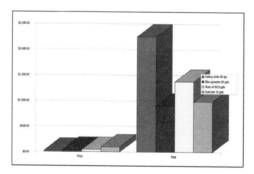

The total amount owed is $5,507.50. We look forward to working with you to close these open invoices.

Sincerely yours,

Abe L. Baker
President

Enc: past due invoices #234, #235, #236, #237

...and the picture gives punch to the words.

The easiest way to control the sizing of the final picture is to insert a frame of the correct size into the document first, if your program offers this feature. Then you can use a special graphics, tools or formatting function to either crop (trim), shrink or enlarge the picture within the frame.

For true text and graphics integration that permits easy layering of the elements, a page composition program is the best.

> **The Flip Side of Clip Art.** *Have you noticed? Everyone has access to the same pictures—the mail box, the little truck...*

Using a desktop laser scanner, a machine much like a copier, you can scan pictures to illustrate your text, or even make a likeness of your signature. However, unlike most ordinary copiers, you drive the scanner from your keyboard with a software program, so you follow the same basic steps any application requires: *define, command, accept.*

Before you begin the scan, write your name in black ink three times on a sheet of white paper. (Make sure the paper isn't too soft or the ink will spread.) Leave plenty of white space around each signature.

Now scan the page:

1. Put the paper face down on the glass of your scanner (or feed it into the document feeder).

2. Start a preview scan.
   Make adjustments to the brightness and contrast, if necessary.

3. Choose the best example of your signature.

4. Isolate that example (usually by stretching a box around it with the cursor).

5. Start the final scan of the selected area.

6. Save it to a new file.

The signature is saved as a .TIF or .TIFF file for many desktop scanners unless you specify another format.

> **High-Density Handwriting.** *If the quality of the electronic signature isn't good enough, try scanning an oversized original (sign it in large strokes) and reducing the size of the picture in your document.*

To use the signature in a word processing document:

1. Open the letter to be signed.

2. Set the cursor at the signature line.

3. Insert a frame, if you like.

4. Import the picture of your signature.

5. Save it in the letter.

When you print the letter, it's already signed.

Micael Angelo

Even if you're out of town, you can sign your letters.

Typography: Plugged-in Style

Word processing resembles typing only in the way that jets resemble biplanes. Today, it turns your PC into a quasi-typesetting machine. This is the foremost capability that has caught the public's fancy.

Typewriters produce monospacing; every letter is the same width. Word processing programs can produce either monospaced or proportional type. A proportional type W is about five times wider than an i. The monospace W and i take up virtually the same space.

Fixed/Proportional Type.

```
This is 12-point monospace (fixed spacing).
```

This is 12-point proportional type (elastic spacing).

Of course, electronic typewriters can produce proportional type of sorts, but word processors add the extra refinement of individual character spacing. Page composition programs and some word processors can produce special electronic file formats for output by a device capable of resolutions of 2540 dots per inch and higher, compared with the common office laser printer at 300- or 600-dpi. The line between typesetting and desktop publishing has all but disappeared.

A respected Boston University study[4] showed that typeset-quality documents were read up to 27% faster than typewritten pages, and that the faster reading speed did not degrade understanding. In that same study, 78% of the readers surveyed found typeset-quality documents to be more professional and 67% found them more credible. More than half the respondents found the typeset documents to be more persuasive.

> **Period.** *The typist's convention of two spaces after the period was invented to make monospacing more readable. The availability of proportional type has given rise to the use of the typesetter's convention of one space after the period.*

Emphasis: Are you still using underlining or FULL CAPS for emphasis? A word typed in capital letters is more difficult to read and slows down the fast-moving eye because the outline of each character is less distinct than its lower-case counterpart. Word processors emphasize with *typestyles:* bold or italic, or contrasting type, and given the right printer, even color. The closer the reader's eye stays to the baseline (the line the character rests on), the faster and easier the information can be read and assimilated.

> **Your Underline is Showing.** *In typesetting, an underline in the manuscript is a call for italic type.*

Underlining text for emphasis or to indicate a title betrays your devotion to the past. Italic type in place of underlining gives a more elegant, contemporary look.

---

4 *Empirical Comparison of the Effectiveness of Typeset, Typewritten and Dot Matrix Business Documents, 1984.* Commissioned by Compugraphic Corporation

Be very sparing with that popular form of emphasis, boldface—too much, and your letter looks merely disorganized or hysterical.

> ***Too Bold for Words.***
> *If **everything** is **important, nothing** is.*

The only excuse for a second font in a standard business letter is to call attention to something out of the ordinary, like a quoted passage. Use a serif, or roman, font such as Times Roman or Palatino for a formal business letter. (A serif is the fine stroke or hook finishing off the main stroke of a letter that draws your eye along to the next letter.) For a more casual look, use a sans serif, or gothic, face like Helvetica or Avant Garde.

The safest type change for beginners is from roman to gothic type or the reverse.

> ***Serif/ Sans Serif (roman or gothic).***
> Serif type makes small letters easier to read.
> **SANS SERIF TYPE IS GOOD FOR HEADINGS.**

Most conventional typewriters offer one typeface, or at best, a limited number, and on some machines changing typefaces is anything but automated. (In the olden days, a daisy wheel on the printer was changed to get a new typeface and style). With a word processor and a laser printer, you can choose from an abundant library of typefaces, in many sizes and weights, as easily as ordering lunch at a deli.

APRIL 1, 1996

Dear *F*riend,

Let me introduce the **Acme Company**, the
leading manufacturer of **Gizmos** in the USA.

Here at ACME CORPORATION we are *pleased* to
send you this one-time S P E C I A L
nontransferable *coupon* for a **$5.00**
discount on our new product.

ACT NOW!!

Yours very truly,

The Ransom Note

So many choices can be both a gift and a curse. In the wrong hands, unlimited fonts and typestyles can make a letter look like a ransom note.

Judicious use of italic type for emphasis can be effective in a business letter; don't overdo it.

A few more guidelines:

- Use type purposefully.

- Change fonts only when it's meaningful to use an alternative.

- Make the change decisively, with enough contrast to be easily noticed by the untrained eye.

- For a business letter, use just one typeface in the text. Nothing betrays your amateur status as quickly as over-decorating your documents with huge bold headlines and fancy fontwork.

- Save mixed-font documents for your sales literature or long documents. Then the contrast between text size and captions, or serif and sans serif type, is useful, not distracting.

That's a beginning to using your PC to improve the way your business communications look. (Check the *Reference* for a list of books you may need to go further.)

But what about making them actually communicate? Let's start with an ordinary business letter.

Letter Perfect

Voice mail, e-mail and the fax might appear to be replacing conventional mail, but in fact, they merely supplement it. Today more people have learned the importance of staying in touch and even v-, e- and f-mail are suffering from overload. Some people pick up their voice mail only when it gets full, and download only the e-mail they're waiting for, leaving unsolicited messages to be deleted automatically when they expire.

People still tend to share important information the way they always have— on paper. The business letter is still your most likely first contact with a new prospect. It must present a picture of authenticity and credibility.

Whether you use a word processor, a typewriter or a quill pen, to write an effective business letter you have to think about content and structure. What do you want to say, how should you say it and how should your letter present it to your reader? Begin with content—well thought out, organized and interesting.

Content

Content means far more than filling up a page with words. The key word is clarity—your first and last concern. Have you said what you mean? Is it easy to understand?

Get Organized

First, tell your reader why you're writing. Then tell why the letter should be read. If you're answering a question, put your answer as near the beginning of the letter as possible. Explain, with your strongest idea, why your offer or request is worthy of attention. Before the closer, use your second strongest idea to leave a sharp impression.

Fuzzy writing comes from fuzzy thinking. To sharpen your writing, focus on your objective before you plunge into your letter. For most people, this six-step process can help:

1. Ask yourself, "Why am I writing?" Reduce the reason—the trigger—to one phrase and you've taken a big step toward organizing your letter.

> **Trigger.** *Newspaper notice of a former client taking a new job in a new industry.*

2. Describe the outcome you want in one short phrase. What is this letter supposed to accomplish? (Make sure the objective is achievable.)

> **Outcome.** *Reintroduce our company and get an appointment.*

3. List the factors contributing to a successful outcome.

> ### Success Factors:
> ■ *Our past working relationship...*
>
> ■ *Our track record in the industry...*
>
> ■ *A special limited-time discount...*
>
> ■ *We're the recognized experts in...*
>
> ■ *A great new product...*

4. Sort your contributing factors by descending importance.

5. Ask yourself, "Why should anyone read this?" and give your list one more critical review.

6. Last, organize these parts in outline form.

What do readers care about most? Themselves, if they're human beings. If you can open with anything that relates to them directly, you've captured their attention.

> **Tell Me More.** *Dear Harry, I saw your picture in the News and thought you'd like an extra copy.*

What background information do you have to include to make your key points credible? Plan each point and use your best ideas as the middle paragraphs of the letter.

Quality, Not Quantity

Q: How long should a letter be?

A: Long enough to get the message across, but brief enough to hold the reader's attention. Most first drafts are too long. No matter how much you think you've pruned, there's usually more to cut. If it's hard to leave out some of your great ideas, just focus on the fact that nothing will be remembered (or even read) if there is too much. Fine-tune your letter. Pare it to the bone, then cut it again and watch your compelling message jump off the page.

> **Writer, Edit Thyself.** *Editing begins at the document level, then by sentence, and only then by word.*

Just as no amount of mustard can hide the absence of meat in a sandwich, no linguistic acrobatics or padding can disguise a thin message. You have about three seconds to engage the reader, so don't waste it on noise.

> **Extraneous Decoration:**
> *In order to...*
> *Do not hesitate to call...*
> *Thanking you in advance...*
> *At this point in time...*
> *If I can be of further assistance...*

Style

In his excellent book *On Writing Well*, William Zinsser pokes holes in the common fallacy that formal writing requires a special, different tone—that, somehow, three-dollar words are better than one-syllable words, and that it's a sin to use a contraction. Zinsser comes down squarely on the side of clarity and simplicity.

There's that word *clarity* again. When you try to impress the reader with your expository skill, your message is buried under all those ten-pound words. Today, the rule is talk to your reader. Tell your story simply and directly. Push your ego out of the way and just say it. The tone of a business letter is formal—you're usually not writing to a close personal friend—but not wooden. It's all right to say *you* and *I.*

Personalizing your business letters makes you more human and warms the reader toward you and your company. Just because people work for an institution, says Zinsser, doesn't mean they have to write like one. Institutional writing is rife with passive voice, clichés, BusinessSpeak and padding. The effect is what some people call "MEGO" (My Eyes Glaze Over).

Syntax

Psycholinguists and cognitive psychologists have found that long sentences strain the average reader's short-term memory. Sentences that are too short are choppy and equally tiring. Ideally, you will develop a rhythm of your own that varies the length of your sentences to maintain the interest level and reduce fatigue. Another barrier to understanding is what's called propositional density. Too many ideas crammed into one sentence make it impossible to understand and retain.

"Watch out for sentences interrupted or overcomplicated by dashes, ellipses or parentheses. Are you trying to combine too many ideas or over-decorating a simple one?"[4]

It's all too easy to pick up bad habits from newspapers, television, radio, and especially the business letters you receive. It is not necessary to adopt a stuffy tone to be businesslike—in fact it marks you as terribly out of date. Clear and simple is best.

Do your best to comb these indignities out of your prose:

- Jargon ("The technical terminology or characteristic idiom of a special…group."[5])

- Pretentious language

- Extraneous embellishment (use one adjective, not two)

- Today's business buzzword (paradigm is a recent offender)

- Legalese (the aforementioned agreement)

---

4 *Writer's Style Guide,* © 1991, 1995 Benchmark Publications Inc.
5 *Webster's Ninth New Collegiate Dictionary*

- Foreign words or phrases, especially Latin (ergo)

- Lazy abbreviations (etc., e.g., i.e.)

If you can't say it out loud without stumbling, don't use it in a letter. Simple words are more powerful than pretentious ones (*use* is crisper than *utilize*, for example). In principle, "Write as you speak" is good advice. In practice, "Write as you speak—if you could go back and edit what you say" is better.

> **Time and the Writer.** *There's a common misconception that professional writers can dash off a page of sparkling prose in minutes. In truth, a good writer often takes hours or even days to polish a single page. The good news is you can recycle any really good writing you produce.*

Repetition

Repetition is a much misunderstood writing device. (Some over-zealous editors cross out every instance of repeated words or phrases regardless of the context.) Used carefully, repetition can serve as reinforcement of a vital point.

Used carelessly, repetition is sloppy writing. Use it only as a deliberate device to underscore your strongest ideas. Check a few pieces of your business mail to see how often the same words are repeated. You'll be amazed at how lazy some writers are with so many words in the language to choose from.

Structure

After you're satisfied with your message, consider how it should take shape on the page.

Along with the main text, good business letters contain certain standard information—date, inside address, salutation, signature block and notations, and sometimes a subject or reference line. Take the elements appropriate for your business and develop them into a standard letter format for everyone in the office to use. Correspondence will have a consistent look.

Inside address: It costs very little to call a company to find out a person's correct title, and using it is a mark of courtesy that yields big dividends.

> **Inside Address.**
> *Mr. Michael Angelo*
> *Vice President, Facilities*
> *Sistine Systems, Inc.*
> *P.O. Box 1110*
> *Rome, New York 13440-1110*

Salutation: How well do you know your reader? Is it Dear Ms. Smith or Dear Leslie? Maybe you only know the addressee as L. E. Smith. If you can't find out the gender of your correspondent before you write, it's better to write *Dear L. E. Smith* or *Dear Leslie Smith* than to guess wrong.

In writing to an organization, Gentlemen or Dear Sirs (unless you know your audience is all male) betrays your ignorance of today's business manners. Some people use *Dear Sir or Madam* or even *Dear Sir/Madam*. Others have gone to great lengths to show their EEO-consciousness with such precious turns of phrase as *Gentlepersons* or *Ladies and Gentlemen*. If you find the perfect way to address a mixed audience, please let us all know!

Subject or reference line: For standard business correspondence, use an attention or reference line only if you are responding to a specific matter such as a purchase order or legal subject.

> **Subject or Reference Line.**
> *Mr. Michael Angelo*
> *Vice President, Facilities*
> *Sistine Systems, Inc.*
> *P.O. Box 1110*
> *Rome, New York 13440-1110*
>
> *Re: PO #234 for 90 Gals Ceiling White*

Signature block: Finish with your name and title. The subject, tone and recipient of the letter will dictate how you take your leave. Today, many business letter writers sign off with *Cordially* to relative strangers. *Regards* go to people they know better, and *Best* [or *Warm*] *regards* are reserved for people they know well. Of course, you can't go wrong with *Sincerely yours.* Above all, be natural and don't stretch for an effect. The stretch marks usually show.

Notation: Some notation conventions are intraoffice conveniences such as the initials that identify the person who typed the letter (for praise or blame, presumably). Today it is more and more common to see a document identifier instead, to aid in finding a computer-generated letter in an electronic filing system.

■ The word *Enclosure:* or Enc: below the signature and initials alerts the reader to look for enclosures. As an added courtesy, list the enclosures so if anything is missing it can be replaced.

- The letters *cc:* used to mean carbon copies are to be sent to the names listed. Today, copies are made on a copier or a printer, so the new trend is to use c: alone.

- Use *Distribution:* and a list (always alphabetic!) if you're sending more than three or four copies.

- If your enclosures don't fit in a standard envelope, use the word *Attachments* at the bottom of the letter and list the documents you're sending. Your recipient will know if anything is missing and you'll have a record of what went to whom.

Outside address: What goes on the envelope? Obviously the name and address, but do you include the honorific (Mr., Ms.)? Some companies do, but it can lead to problems with good old Leslie. It's perfectly acceptable to address business mail without it, but it is less formal. Some forward thinkers use M. alone as the honorific for ambiguous names.

- The simplest envelope format is the return address (always!), name, address, ZIP code (always!) and a stamp. The *Delivery* chapter shows where that gets you.

- Two important parts of the address are omitted all too often: the title and the mail stop. The mail stop is essential in writing to someone in a large company. The bigger the corporation, the bigger the black hole for misdirected mail. It isn't hard to find out this information.

Whatever you decide about the way you address your mail, be consistent. Set a standard for your company and stick to it.

Layout

The cleanest look for a business letter is left-aligned (block left), from the address block down through the signature. If you don't like it or it doesn't work with your letterhead, try modified block left (everything lines up at the left except for the date and the signature block).

You've seen page layouts with the date out in right field and the signature somewhere in the center infield—not a pretty sight. Anyone can do plain block left without training and it always looks reasonably uniform.

Use block paragraphs (indentations in business correspondence went out of style long ago). Add extra leading between paragraphs. Leading is the term for the more precise line spacing available with typographic letter forms. Keep your paragraphs short. Nothing is more forbidding than a mass of unrelieved gray space.

GE **GE Plastics**

Plastics Technology Division
General Electric Company
One Plastics Ave., Pittsfield, MA 01201
413-448-7110

Month Day, Year

Addressee Name
Addressee Title
Business Name
Street Address
City, State Zip Code
Nation (if applicable)

one-third fold line

The salutation and body of the letter always begin below the top third of the folded letterhead.

For short letters, leave more than three line spaces between the address and salutation.

Salutation:

This typewritten letter demonstrates the approved block left typing format which complements all International GE letterheads.

Each line of typing, including the first line of each paragraph, aligns with the left side of the Monogram. The right margin is a minimum of 25 millimeters, and there is one line space between each paragraph.

The date and the address block are positioned in the top third of the folded letterhead, with the salutation below the fold. To create this arrangement, type the date nine lines below the red line and leave one line space between the date and the address block. Leave three line spaces between the address block and the salutation, and leave one line space between the salutation and the first line of the letter.

At the end of the letter, leave one line space above the complimentary close, and four line spaces between the complimentary close and the sender's name. Leave two line spaces below the sender's name or title and single space any additional information.

Complimentary Close,

On personalized letterheads, the sender's name and title may be omitted, if desired.

Sender's Name
Sender's Title

SI/ti
enclosure
cc:
First Name
Second Name

An Expert Business Letter Format—Courtesy of General Electric Company

> **Now Hear This.** *To emphasize a point or call attention to a quotation, use a center indent: Both right and left margins are set in equidistant from the margins.*

Short letters present their own formatting problems. They hover at the top of the page too timid to stake out some space, or they float miserably somewhere in the center. Try more space between the letterhead and the date and the body and the closing, or increase the spacing to 1.5 lines. Whatever you do, don't resort to padding the content to make the letter longer.

To shorten a letter that's too long, divide the information between a letter and one or more longer documents to be attached. To keep the attachments from being orphaned (only to sink by their own weight to the bottom of the in-basket), use a cover sheet or label for each piece. Another solution for short letters is monarch-size stationery, a nice addition to your correspondence toolkit.

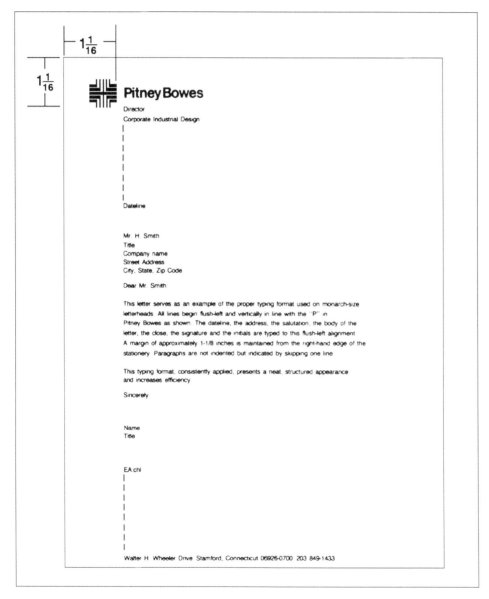

Use monarch stationery for short letters.

—Courtesy of Pitney Bowes, Inc.

Envelope Layout

Use a #10 commercial business envelope for general business correspondence, preferably preprinted with your company's return address. The
delivery address is normally laid out block left, starting two and three-
quarters inches above the bottom edge and extending no closer than five-
eighths of an inch from that edge.

Direct address printing: Printing the receiver's address directly on the
envelope rather than on a label looks personal and important. It's easy to do
for certain envelope sizes. Check your printer manual to see what sizes it
can accept (usually a standard #10, at least). Then check your word
processing program for templates of corresponding sizes.

Labels

If you can't print directly on envelopes, you can buy quite acceptable clear
labels that present almost as formal a look as direct printing. Of course, you
have to use labels if your printer can't print certain sizes, and mailing-size
labels are important for large envelopes. Check *Resources* for low-cost
special equipment for printing labels. Most full-featured word processing
programs provide templates for standard label sizes.

Checklist for Design

✔ Learn from the experts.

✔ Standardize your look.

✔ Use emphasis cautiously.

✔ Keep language clear and direct.

✔ Don't be afraid to try anything your PC can do.

This has been a quick look at the basic elements of design—a few safe ideas that can take your correspondence to a higher level. The next chapter introduces some practical applications of design.

Desktop Marketing

Desktop Marketing

A marketing expert we know said recently, *"Marketing by mail is such a civilized way to do business."*

Direct mail marketing is now a billion-dollar industry. Marketers like direct mail because it's targeted to a specific audience and it's highly action-oriented. You write directly to your reader, aiming for a specific response.

"With direct mail, your promotional dollars are spent more selectively than in any other medium."[1]

In this chapter you'll learn about:

■ Desktop Marketing Practices and Principles

■ Building a Desktop Marketing Startup Kit

■ Putting Special Mailings to good use

But first, let's visit the inventor of direct mail marketing.

1 *How to Grow Your Business Using The Mail,* © 1992 Pitney Bowes, Inc.

Mr. Patterson Discovers the Mail

John H. Patterson, founder of National Cash Register Company (NCR), Dayton, Ohio, is a legend in direct mail marketing. He bought a failing company and set about making it successful, and himself very, very rich. He invented business-to-business mail in 1884.

Patterson called direct mail "The Strong Right Arm of Selling." He used it much the way many companies use it today: to build his company's image and generate qualified leads, in his case for follow-up by his sales agents. Mr. Patterson had a plan to revive his moribund business.

Patterson's Campaign

John Patterson hired ten sales agents all over the country and assigned them the task of finding 500 merchants in their own territories.

Then Old John hired carpenters to build a sorting bin with 18 compartments.

Next, he bought 100,000 envelopes and hired six young men from the local commercial college to address 18 envelopes to each name.

Then John Patterson invented the promotional letter. He wrote 18 different messages, *"all unlike anything used in advertising before. These messages told prospects why they needed the cash register, not why NCR needed the sale."* [2]

---

2 "Lessons from the Rear View Mirror," © 1983, John Yeck

On 18 successive days, Patterson mailed each of his 5,000 prospects a different promotional letter—six days a week for three weeks.

Did it work? In 1887, NCR sales agent Harry Blood wrote to the home office:

> *"Gents...the system is a good one. In Attica, Indiana, I was unable to sell a party [who] I knew needed a register. For a while, I sent him, every day, a circular in [the] mail. The order came back to me right through the mail."*

The mail worked so well for NCR, John mailed almost four million pieces in 1891; five million in 1892 and six million in 1901. Remember, this was before postage meters and word processing.

"It took more than 30 'girls' working steadily all month just to type the addresses." We've come a long way.

Practices and Principles

In the *Design* chapter, you learned about the importance of the structure and appearance of your documents. Your company's personality should be just as easy to recognize. Caterpillar Inc. calls it One Voice:

"The Caterpillar personality is shaped in part by the products we make— hard-working machines and engines often described as 'powerful,' 'strong,' and 'rugged.'… When we speak as a company…it makes sense to use words and visuals that reflect who we are."[3]

Caterpillar encourages communicators to use strong images and active, powerful language to convey the total personality of the company within the corporate identity architecture.

Learn from the experts. Reflect on who you are, what makes your organization unique, and the words and pictures that will tell your story. Develop a voice of your own.

---

3 *Communicating Caterpillar: One Voice,* © 1994 Caterpillar Inc.

Caterpillar products are **down-to-earth,** **straightforward,** **gritty** and **rugged.** The Cat name is **enduring.** To meet our customers' expectations, our products have to be **strong,** **powerful** and **reliable.** We are **genuine** and **accessible** and act as an **honest partner** in our relations with dealers, customers and each other—and we're **responsive** and **global** enough to meet our customers' changing needs. We're **serious,** **thorough** and **professional** about our business, **active** and highly **industrious,** **dedicated** to helping our customers succeed. Our **commanding** engines and machines are of the highest quality, and that is what makes us **competitive** and our industry's **leader.**

How would you define your company's voice?—Courtesy of Caterpillar Inc.

Use a word processor or a desktop publishing (DTP) program to design your mailing pieces. The differences are just matters of degree; word processors are catching up to DTP programs fast.

Still, DTP programs can handle a greater variety of graphics than some word processors, and the greater capability of layering text and graphics can give you more choices in design. DTP programs are also more versatile in handling type, offering finer letter and line spacing than most WP programs and better grayscale and color handling. Most DTP programs can rotate type and graphics in small increments; most WP programs can't.

In any case, it's a good idea to work up to a proficient level on your word processor before stepping up to the next level. With just a word processor, you can build a professional-looking desktop marketing startup kit with these basic components:

- Mailing envelope (the "outer")

- Promotional letter

- Response device

- Brochure or mailer

Start by jotting down exactly what you expect your marketing kit to accomplish. Be very clear and specific about your goal and don't ask too much of one mailing. You'll only confuse your reader.

Most effective direct marketing packages contain the:

- *Offer*, which must answer the WIFM question ("What's in it for me?")

- *Credibility factor*, describing the features and benefits of your product or service

- *Call to action*, or "asking for the order"

Now list the role each piece in the kit will play.

- *Envelope:* Attracts attention, generates curiosity, *gets there on time.*

- *Promotional letter:* Creates excitement, urgency; clearly explains the offer; asks for a response.

- *Response device:* Makes it easy to order; captures customer information.

- *Brochure:* Covers the features and benefits in depth; lends credibility.

- *Mailer:* Serves as a mini-brochure/reply device all in one.

> **Desktop Marketing Pledge.** *We will never, ever send anything anywhere without our company name, address and phone number on every important piece.*

There's an old direct mail adage that you can't keep a reader too busy or supply too much detail. That may be true, but what you provide must be carefully organized to guide your reader to a decision. The simplest organizing principle is top-down and then sequential. Start with the broadest idea. Then list the steps your reader is supposed to take to respond. Make sure the sequence is clear and logical.

Desktop Marketing Startup Kit

You know your business better than anyone, and that knowledge is more valuable than design talent in developing a marketing packet that tells your story.

Try a little role-play before you go on. Take an obvious marketing mailing piece out of your in-basket. Quick! What do you notice first? Does the outside envelope make you want to open it or throw it away?

Now open it and study the way the components are assembled. Do you know what you're supposed to look at first? Now read each piece. Do you know what you're supposed to do when you've read everything? When your own mailing kit is complete, make sure your readers give the right answers to these questions.

Here are some ideas on what to put in—or on—each component of your desktop marketing kit to get your creative juices flowing. Remember to apply the design principles discussed earlier to give your kit an instantly recognizable family look.

Mailing Envelope

Look at the outside of the package. Most direct mail hits the recipient's wastebasket unopened. What would make you open this envelope, slit the wrapper or unfasten the box? (Which ones *do* you open?)

> ***Cover the Bases.*** *When you design your envelope, use all of your real estate. Plan both the white space and the printed part.*

A teaser on the envelope draws the reader in. *"Become independently wealthy in 10 days!"* is a grabber for a certain type of reader. *"A one-time offer for only the most discerning"* speaks to a different person entirely. Whether or not the envelope is opened depends on how well the teaser defines the target.

The envelope should say, "Good deal!" "Just for me!" "What is this?" "Important!" in a tone that matches the target audience. Be careful here. As with type and typestyles, too much is…too much. It's been said that an envelope that says too much is weaker than one that says nothing at all.

Here are some excellent examples of simple, yet powerful teasers that make you want to open the package.

Pitney Bowes

40 Lindeman Drive
Trumbull CT 06611-4785

PRESORTED
FIRST CLASS

ROCHESTER
NOV 24'93
N.Y.

PB METER
7153721

≡ 0.24 8

U.S. POSTAGE

WOW!

Save $2,500
on your mailing costs
RIGHT NOW!

GUARANTEED!

5LB074SG 041 007
MR. SAMPLE
ABC COMPANY
123 ANY STREET
ANYTOWN US 12345-6789

An Expert Outer—Courtesy of Pitney Bowes, Inc.

WOW! This program had a sales close rate of over forty percent.

It's important not to tell your whole story on the outside. That gives your reader a chance to decide not to be interested even before reading your entire message.

Another Expert Outer—Courtesy of SNET

This SNET direct mail campaign exceeded the company's expectations by about 200% in the first year. (It may be coincidence, but some marketing experts believe the best outer is any kind of a box. People open boxes.)

Plan the outer from the inside out. You should know exactly what is going inside and to whom it will be mailed before you decide on the quality of the paper stock.

An upscale target requires high-quality stock such as fine vellum. A soft color—perhaps ivory—lends a classic look. This choice would be all wrong if your target is the great bargain-hunting public. Look into craft paper envelopes and vivid colors. (See *Reference* for likely resources for appropriate "outers.")

Direct Marketing Letter

"When mailing to produce a lead, a sale or store traffic, in tests that pit a self-mailer or printed card against a plain letter in an envelope, the letter-in-envelope invariably wins."[4]

The direct marketing promotional letter is significantly different from a standard business letter. With any kind of letter, you're selling your company. The direct marketing letter is more frankly promotional and is likely to be selling a product, service or event rather than just introducing a corporation or institution.

In designing your promotional letter, use the same six steps you used for your business letter:

1. Why am I writing?

2. What outcome do I want?

3. What are my success factors?

4. What are the most important points?

5. Why would anyone read this?

6. Start with an outline.

The next few pages offer tips on writing your marketing letter, based on recent research and the authors' collective years of experience.

---

4 John D. Yeck, Yeck Brothers Group, Dayton, Ohio

> *A Johnson box is often used to introduce
> the subject in a promotional letter.*

■ Enclosing text in a Johnson box calls attention to it and draws the reader's eye to your message. The Johnson box can be effective for a special offer. Be sure the tone matches your target audience.

> ***Johnson Box.*** *On a typewriter, producing a Johnson box once meant laboriously typing asterisks around the copy. On some word processors, the Johnson box is a snap. Type the text, select the Format or Tools menu, choose a border style and you're finished.*

■ Place important messages strategically.

   "Make your offer the focal point, the place your eye can't miss."[5]

■ Structure the information in a logical sequence. Look at it from the top down, and then in descending order of detail. Your brochure will contain the same information in different words.

■ You can take more liberty in text decoration in a promotional letter, but don't overdo it.

5 *How to Grow Your Business Using The Mail*

- Keep the classic AIDA principles in mind:

> **A**ttention
> **I**nterest
> **D**esire
> **A**ction

- *Personalize:* A personalized letter tells your reader "You are not a faceless, anonymous number," but don't let the seams of your device show. Use some imagination in choosing what to plug in to the letter. "All you folks on Fillintheblank Street" has been worked to death; too much of this kind of thing can make you look phony.

  See *Production* for step-by-step instructions for personalizing your promotional letters automatically on your PC.

- Close with a *call to action*, preferably with some urgency. "To order, please return the postage-free business reply card before May 15..." or "Supplies are limited so call early for your free booklet...."

- The *postscript* is reported to hold one of the most important places in a marketing letter. The postscript is to attract the readers' interest and perhaps induce them to reread the letter. Most people read a postscript, often before they read anything else.

  A P.S. shouldn't be an afterthought. Use it to restate your offer, or to include an inducement to act now.

  The postscript belongs in the sales letter, but not in a formal business letter.

P.S. Call Now!

⊞ PitneyBowes

40 Lindeman Drive
Trumbull, CT 06611-4785

....
SAVE ON THE UPCOMING USPS RATE INCREASE
WITH ONE OF 3 SOFT-GUARD® RATE PROTECTION PLANS
....

Dear Customer:

The United States Postal Service has filed for a postage rate increase for early 1995. Updating the database in your 5 lb. scale costs on average $195 *per change*. **To help you reduce costs, Pitney Bowes has designed 3 SOFT-GUARD® RATE PROTECTION PLANS**. One should be the perfect alternative for your office:

1. ECONOMY PLAN (JUST $95 ANNUALLY) - This basic SOFT-GUARD® PLAN is designed for customers who primarily use 1st class and priority rates and occasionally 3rd class rates. You would be entitled to receive **new updated rate specific software UP TO 2 TIMES PER YEAR**. On the upcoming USPS rate change alone, it can save you $100! And the plan offers one additional software update. If you don't use ZIP® to Zone conversions, international rates and USPS Express Mail, this plan is ideal for you.

2. MULTI-YEAR PLAN (JUST $145 ANNUALLY — GUARANTEED FOR 3 YEARS — A $135 SAVINGS OFF THE STANDARD PLAN) - This SOFT-GUARD® PLAN offers a major discount for those who want to lock in long-term service protection. You would be entitled to receive **new rate specific software UP TO 3 TIMES PER YEAR** if there are *USPS rate changes, ZIP®/Zone changes, geographical expansions/changes, international rate changes and Express Mail changes.*

3. STANDARD PLAN ($190 ANNUALLY FOR FULL COVERAGE) - With this SOFT-GUARD® PLAN, you would be entitled to receive **new rate specific software UP TO 6 TIMES PER YEAR** if there are *USPS rate changes, ZIP®/Zone changes, geographical expansions/changes, international rate changes and Express Mail changes.*

Join the other Pitney Bowes customers who have insured over 97,000 machines with the SOFT-GUARD® RATE PROTECTION PLAN. Your personalized agreement is enclosed. Just check off the Plan that's best for your office, then sign and return the agreement. Your SOFT-GUARD® Rate Protection Plan will go into effect immediately. Any questions? Call us at **1-800-MR BOWES (1-800-672-6937) and ask for Program 2811**. We're here to serve you.

Sincerely,

Archie A. Martin, Vice President
Customer Service

P.S. **I urge you to act before the date printed on your agreement form** — your savings on the upcoming USPS rate change can be significant!

An Expert Promotional Letter—Courtesy of Pitney Bowes, Inc.

- You might create special stationery to use rather than your regular formal letterhead. Colored paper with a special slogan added to your company name and address works well for an informal promotion.

- Either hand-sign your letters, or sign a master copy before printing.

- PC-generated business mail can include a genuine handwritten signature digitized on a scanner and incorporated into the document file.

- You can also simulate handwritten notes by scanning them in as pictures, slanted for a casual afterthought look. If you can print your note in another color, all the better.

Reply Device

How should you invite your reader to respond to your message—mail, fax, store coupon or phone? Fax and phone offer speed and immediacy, but they have certain disadvantages. Fax machines are not yet universally available and phone responses will alienate callers if you don't have the staff to handle them. Interest in your product will drop as the busy signals rise.

Telephone responses take more staff time and considerably more effort to capture important details. Mail is an excellent medium for getting replies if you make it easy for your readers to respond.

Here are some other tips for effective reply generators:

- Restate your offer on the reply form. Remember, it gets separated from the rest of the package.

- Give exact directions to assure faster, more accurate fulfillment.

- Never enclose a stamped envelope or loose postage. If the prospect doesn't bite, you've just wasted the money with no return on your investment.

Now for a limited time!

THE MOST COST-EFFICIENT, PRODUCTIVE AND FLEXIBLE MAIL PROCESSOR IN THE WORLD COMES WITH $2,500 WORTH OF POSTAGE – OR A $2,500 LEASE CREDIT.

No other system is so advanced in ways to save you time and money.

And if you order the Pitney Bowes PARAGON™ Mail Processor by December 31, 1993, we'll put $2,500 worth of postage in your POSTAGE BY PHONE® account – absolutely free! Or we'll give you a credit of $2,500 toward your lease. Return this postage-paid response card today, or, for faster service, call 1-800-MR BOWES (1-800-672-6937), and ask for Ext. 3263 to learn more about how PARAGON can put you way ahead of the rest. Offer ends December 31, 1993.

YES!

I want to revolutionize my mailroom and get $2,500 worth of postage FREE or a $2,500 lease credit.

Please call me at this number:

(_____) _____ - _____ Ext. _____

```
00327859005
MANAGER MAILING OPERATIONS
BOSTON FINANCIAL DATA
SERVICES INC
260 VICTORY RD
QUINCY, MA 02171
```

Contact Name: _____

Title: _____

DM 3263

Restate the offer.—Courtesy of Pitney Bowes, Inc.

If you've enclosed your offer with a billing statement and the recipient is likely to respond anyway, enclose a self-addressed courtesy reply envelope or card. All your customer has to do is put on the stamp. A ready-to-mail piece is almost as good as free postage.

Bounceback. *Check the typeface on the response address in the picture. Notice it's in italic type. More about this in* Delivery.

Quality points – On a scale of 1 to 5 (5 is the highest), rate each entry in the five categories: Discovering, Planning, Selecting, Installing and Training.

Discovering: Please rate these sources of information about CentraLink (how informative? how useful to your decision in choosing CentraLink?):

SNET AUTHORIZED REPRESENTATIVE	5	4	3	2	1
PRINT ADVERTISEMENT	5	4	3	2	1
RADIO ADVERTISEMENT	5	4	3	2	1
DIRECT MAIL: BROCHURE	5	4	3	2	1
VIDEO	5	4	3	2	1
OTHER _____	5	4	3	2	1
(please specify)					

Planning: Please rate your planning resources.

CENTRALINK SYSTEM PLANNER	5	4	3	2	1
SNET AUTHORIZED REPRESENTATIVE	5	4	3	2	1
OTHER _____	5	4	3	2	1

SUGGESTED IMPROVEMENTS: _____

Selecting: Please rate your selection criteria.

SNET RELIABILITY	5	4	3	2	1
LINE-AT-A-TIME GROWTH	5	4	3	2	1
CENTRAL OFFICE TECH SUPPORT	5	4	3	2	1
FEATURES	5	4	3	2	1
COST	5	4	3	2	1
OTHER _____	5	4	3	2	1

SUGGESTED IMPROVEMENTS: _____

Installing: Please rate the quality of SNET installation service.

ON TIME	5	4	3	2	1
COURTEOUS	5	4	3	2	1
THOROUGH	5	4	3	2	1
LEFT THE SITE NEAT AND CLEAN	5	4	3	2	1
OTHER _____	5	4	3	2	1

SUGGESTED IMPROVEMENTS: _____

Training: Please rate your training resources.

CENTRALINK TRAINING VIDEO	5	4	3	2	1
DESKTOP GUIDE	5	4	3	2	1
QUICKCARD	5	4	3	2	1
CENTRALINK SYSTEM GUIDE	5	4	3	2	1
SNET AUTHORIZED REPRESENTATIVE	5	4	3	2	1
OTHER _____	5	4	3	2	1

SUGGESTED IMPROVEMENTS: _____

What other systems did you consider? _____

Other suggestions or comments: _____

Thank you for your help.

NAME _____

TITLE _____

FIRM _____

TELEPHONE _____

ADDRESS _____

CITY _____ ST _____ ZIP _____

NUMBER OF CENTRALINK LINES _____

NUMBER OF NON-SNET TELEPHONES _____

BRAND NAMES _____

MODEL NUMBERS _____

Let your reply device do your market research.—Courtesy of SNET

■ Make your reply forms do double-duty as market researchers. Any form filled in by your reader is the most reliable way to track the effectiveness of your direct marketing material. The information your customers give you is worth a hundred times more than any you can get secondhand. Listen to the people who are actually buying your product.

- Use a postpaid reply device with a preprinted imprint as an added inducement for a reply. You pay outbound postage, but inbound postage is charged only for responses that are mailed by your target.

- You can also meter your response device if expense isn't an issue. Turn off the date so your prospects can return the card or envelope any time. You pay for each piece whether or not it's returned.

The *Production* chapter gives generic step-by-step instructions for preparing an envelope on your PC. See the *Delivery* chapter for more on reply devices.

Brochure

The letter and brochure or mailer should contain the same basic information, yet each should be able to stand alone. Start with your six-step plan, then add a seventh step to your construction process. Lay out every topic by page, paying attention to the sequence in which the reader will unfold and read the contents.

- Apply your standard brochure grid to give the publication underlying strength. Then use your outlined points to decide where each idea goes.

- The brochure will make the same key points as the letter, but will expand each idea, especially in the features and benefits department.

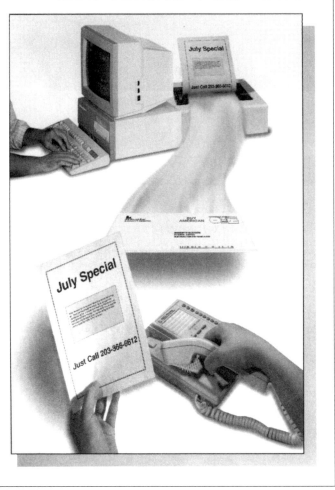

An Expert Brochure—Courtesy of Pitney Bowes, Inc.

- Use folios (page numbers) if page order isn't evident. Folios can be at the top or bottom (*drop* folios) of the page, where they are usually positioned at the outside corners on facing pages. Uneven numbers are *recto* or right pages—the number goes on the outer right corner. Left pages are *verso*—the number goes on the outer left corner.

- Trust your readers to be smart enough to find their way around your document. They have been conditioned throughout their lives to read sequentially. You don't need signposts to tell them to turn to page 2 when they get to the bottom of page 1. They'll figure it out.

The expert brochure is being used by nearly 10,000 businesses in the U.S. alone.

Mailer

The obvious advantages of a mailer over a brochure are economy and convenience. A mailer can be designed to fit in a #10 envelope. A tri-fold two-sided mailer gives you six pages to say a lot and still get a free ride with your letter for an ounce of postage. If you include a *bounceback* (a perforated tear-off reply device) you may have to use a heavier card stock.

On their own, mailers can be low-cost, all-in-one letter-brochure-reply devices. Mailers work well for an association announcement, a meeting notice, a compact direct marketing piece or a product offering. You can buy mailer paper preprinted and prescored for folding. All you have to do is add your own words and pictures. Software templates are also available to help you set up your text and graphics to fit the preprinted sheets correctly, something like the electronic grids the Caterpillar designers use. Practice on plain paper first!

See the *Reference* section for more sources for pre-designed, perforated mailer stock.

Here are some mailer ideas that might work for you:

Expert Mailer Options—Courtesy of Paper Direct, Inc.

A Complete Marketing Kit—Courtesy of SNET

Special Mailings

Your customers want to hear from you. Some marketing sources say your mail should hit their desks at least six times a year. Others say *once a month*. Are you ready to handle that volume? Do you have enough new and interesting things to mail to your customers?

Consider this: It's been shown that of all the direct marketing mail people receive, the pieces most likely to be opened or at least noticed are from companies they already know. Don't you pay more attention to the mail you get from people you already do business with?

Marketing is a relationship-building activity. To keep your company in your customers' minds and forge stronger bonds with them, there are several other ways to use the mails when you need something new to send.

> ***Help!*** *You may decide to use outside resources to keep your customers happy and focus your attention on new business. Remember, you're out to grow your business, not recycle it. See the* Reference *for ideas about outsourcing.*

Postcards

Here are some reasons for using postcards as stand-alone communiqués:

- Who can resist a postcard? Almost everyone at least glances at them. That gives you a precious split second to attract attention to your message.

- They're low-cost. A postcard is about 8 to 10 cents cheaper than a First-Class letter, depending on the number of pieces sent at one time.

- They're especially well-suited to acknowledgments, announcements or reminders.

- Postcards are useful for cleaning lists before mailing expensive pieces.

Double-sided postcards cost a little more, but they may have an edge in getting readers to respond. One side presents your message; the other is a detachable business reply card.

Be sure to check the *Delivery* chapter for Postal Service requirements for postcards. They can be a little tricky.

An Expert Postcard—Courtesy of the U.S. Postal Service

Newsletters

Newsletters are versatile and effective communications tools. They can be a profitable product in themselves, sold by subscription. A good newsletter is a goodwill ambassador; it builds a relationship between your company and your customers. At the same time, it can function as direct mail in disguise— as a vehicle to pitch products and services subtly while keeping customers up to date with trends and developments. In some cases, newsletters serve all three purposes at once. (Purists frown on using newsletters to sell products. Typically, a newsletter that lives up to its name does not carry advertising.)

If you plan to sell subscriptions to your newsletter, these tips may be useful:[6]

- Don't overestimate the number of people who will subscribe to your publication. [It would be wise to test the market with an inquiry card first.]

- Keep the premise simple. If you can't describe the theme "in 25 words or less," it's too complicated.

- Plan a reasonable test period. Most successful newsletters are published at least once a month, so just don't try a few sample issues.

- The reader is interested in what you have to say. Make your publication attractive, but don't overdesign it.

The most common newsletter format is two or four pages, although the more elaborate subscription publications often run much longer. Shorter newsletters are normally folded in half or thirds, with the address and

---

6 Source: The Newsletter Publishers Association

postage placed on an outside panel. Even the simplest computer-generated newsletters can offer plenty of eye appeal, thanks to desktop publishing or advanced word processing.

Many software programs provide good-looking templates that take the novice a long way toward a professional publication. These templates point the way to balancing drawings and text, and give you predefined heads and subheads and other design elements. If you can, customize the template you choose to make your publication distinctive.

You can attach a mailing label directly to the outside of your newsletter or use a standard envelope or an outside wrapper. If you can print directly on the newsletter, that's even better. See *Delivery* for mailing rules for newsletters.

A few basic guidelines will give your newsletter an extra measure of credibility.

- Include a masthead, the section that lists the company publisher, editors, outside credits and copyright information. The masthead generally runs in a box on the inside front page.

- Include a table of contents if the newsletter is more than four pages. A boxed TOC on the cover or even the outside fold can be effective as a teaser.

Newsletter

Heading 1

Lorem ipsum dolor sit amet, consectetuer adipiscing elit, sed diam nonummy nibh euismod tincidunt ut laoreet dolore magna aliquam erat volutpat. Ut wisi enim ad minim veniam, quis nostrud exerci tation ullamcorper suscipit lobortis nisl ut aliquip ex ea commodo consequat. Duis autem vel eum iriure dolor in hendrerit in vulputate velit esse molestie consequat, vel illum dolore eu feugiat nulla facilisis at vero eros et accumsan et iusto odio dignissim qui blandit praesent luptatum zzril delenit augue duis dolore te feugait nulla facilisi.

L orem ipsum dolor sit amet, consectetuer adipiscing elit, sed diam nonummy nibh euismod tincidunt ut laoreet Ut wisi enim ad minim veniam, quis nostrud exerci tation ullamcorper suscipit lobortis nisl ut aliquip ex ea commodo consequat. Duis autem vel eum iriure dolor in hendrerit in vulputate velit esse molestie consequat, vel illum dolore eu feugiat nulla facilisis at vero eros et accumsan et iusto odio dignissim qui blandit praesent luptatum zzril delenit augue duis dolore te feugait nulla facilisi. Lorem

Nam liber tempor cum soluta nobis eleifend option congue.

ipsum dolor sit amet, consectetuer adipiscing elit, sed diam nonummy nibh euismod tincidunt ut laoreet dolore magna aliquam erat volutpat. Ut wisi enim ad minim veniam, quis nostrud exerci tation ullamcorper suscipit lobortis nisl ut aliquip ex ea commodo consequat. Duis autem vel eum iriure

dolor in hendrerit in vulputate velit esse molestie consequat, vel illum dolore eu feugiat nulla facilisis at vero eros et accumsan et iusto odio dignissim qui blandit praesent luptatum zzril delenit augue duis dolore te feugait nulla facilisi. Lorem ipsum dolor sit amet, consectetuer adipiscing elit, sed diam nonummy nibh euismod tincidunt ut laoreet dolore magna aliquam erat volutpat. Ut wisi enim ad minim veniam, quis nostrud exerci tation ullamcorper suscipit lobortis nisl ut aliquip ex ea commodo consequat. Duis autem vel eum iriure dolor in hendrerit in vulputate velit esse molestie consequat, vel illum dolore eu

feugiat nulla facilisis at vero eros et accumsan et iusto odio dignissim qui blandit praesent luptatum zzril delenit augue duis dolore te feugait nulla facilisi. Lorem ipsum dolor sit amet, consectetuer adipiscing elit, sed diam nonummy nibh euismod tincidunt ut laoreet dolore magna aliquam erat volutpat. Ut wisi enim a

Heading 3

Ut wisi enim ad minim veniam, quis nostrud exerci tation ullamcorper suscipit lobortis nisl ut aliquip ex ea commodo consequat. Duis autem vel eum iriure dolor in hendrerit in vulputate velit esse molestie consequat, vel illum dolore eu feugiat nulla facilisis at vero eros et accumsan et iusto odio dignissim qui blandit praesent luptatum zzril delenit augue duis dolore te feugait nulla facilisi. Lorem ipsum dolor sit amet, consectetuer adipiscing elit, sed diam nonummy nibh euismod tincidunt ut laoreet dolore magna aliquam erat volutpat. Ut wisi enim ad minim veniam, quis nostrud exerci tation ullamcorper suscipit lobortis nisl ut aliquip ex ea commodo consequat. Duis autem vel eum iriure dolor in hendrerit in vulputate velit esse molestie consequat, vel illum dolore eu accumsan et iusto odio dignissim qui blandit praesent

CONTENTS

An Expert Newsletter Template (Aldus PageMaker)
—Courtesy of Adobe Systems Corporation

- Be sure you have something to say other than a sales pitch. A newsletter implies *news*. Readers feel defrauded if all they get is your commercial.

- By definition, a newsletter is a periodical. Use a volume and number scheme in the header or footer. The Volume increments yearly; the Number, by issue.

- Copyright it. The copyright information is positioned at the bottom of the inside cover or in the masthead box. Check the front of this book for the standard copyright format.

- Invite your readers to quote from your newsletter as long as they give you a credit line and send you a copy of the issue that runs the quote. It's free publicity.

> **Extra!** *A cross-folded 11- by 17-inch sheet makes a handy self-contained four-page newsletter. Be sure to practice the folds before you make your mechanical.*

Checklist for Desktop Marketing

✔ Find your voice.

✔ Plan your marketing kit from the inside out.

✔ Include the offer, the credibility factor and the call to action in every marketing mailing.

✔ Remember AIDA.

✔ Personalize your marketing offers.

✔ Make it easy for prospects to respond.

✔ Stay in touch with your customers.

✔ Put your company name, address and telephone number on every important piece.

You've decided on what to say and how it should look. Now you have to decide whom to send it to and how to print it.

Production

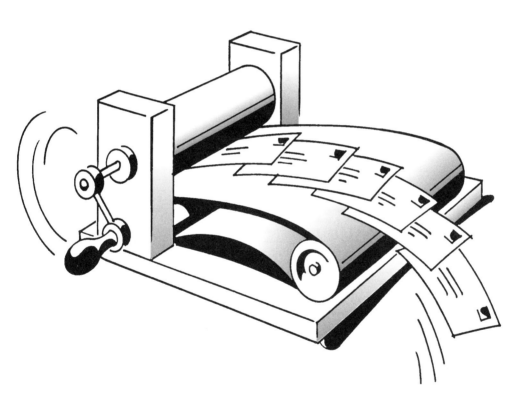

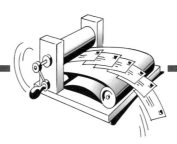

Production

Skeptics in the high tech field are apt to put down a new idea with the comment, "that's a technology looking for an application." Business correspondence, however, is an application that was born screaming for technology. Ever since the first secretary typed the identical letter to three customers, people have been looking for ways to avoid repetitive typing. That's why we invent machines.

PCs offer varying degrees of automating repetitive tasks. Saving chunks of good ideas as boilerplate and assembling them in different combinations for different audiences is a semi-automatic way of producing edited, proofed copy in a hurry. To get several dozen perfect letters quickly, you can save a master letter and just change minor parts like the date and addressee. On the other hand, true automation—generating hundreds of letters without human intervention—calls for a database and a coded document. This chapter follows the trail from the single letter (the "one-off") to real automated business mail:

- Going from One-Offs to Small Batches

- Extending your reach through Mass Appeal

- The Ins and Outs of Printing

- Producing your Desktop Marketing Kit

But first, a brief history of how a technology finally caught up with its application.

The Great American Swiss Army Machine

First came the cord and the plug. The electric typewriting machine (ET) was introduced in 1895, but didn't begin to catch on as a commercial product for almost half a century. In the mid-30s, a new IBM Electromatic typewriter cost about the same as a used car.

The electric typewriter began to overtake the manual machine around the mid-1950s even though the price difference remained high. Players like IBM, Olivetti, Triumph and Adler offered heavy, expensive and by today's standards, somewhat unattractive machines, but they were as welcome to typists as power mowers were to landscapers.

To leverage the electric typewriter's toehold in the office products market, IBM bundled it with its dictation product line, but continued to meet price resistance around the world. In Germany, for example, the ET might cost two to three times the cost of a manual typewriter, and an IBM dictation system could exceed a secretary's annual salary.

To justify these unheard of prices, IBM's sales reps in Germany invented studies to measure the cost of creating text, from the spoken word to the printed page.

Textverarbeitung

The studies originated under the name *Textverarbeitung*—working with text.[1] Surveying a business office from the origin of a document through

---

1 *The Romance Division…A Different Side of IBM,*
  © 1991, DeLoca and Kalow

the revision cycle to the printed piece, it wasn't too difficult to prove that stenography and manual typing were far more costly in terms of productivity (not to mention accuracy) than dictation and electric typing.

Word Processing

The American IBM reps admired this new sales technique and dubbed it *word processing*. In the early '60s, they brought the marketing concept back to the States where eventually the term was applied to the first real electronic "word processing machine," the IBM Magnetic Tape Selectric Typewriter (MTST). The MTST borrowed data processing concepts to use magnetic tape for recording and replaying typed information. This $10,000 electronic typing machine brought true automation to the secretarial pool.

The next evolutionary step was to the memory typewriter (limited storage, reliable medium) and magnetic card machines (unlimited storage, relatively fragile medium). The biggest leap forward was the addition of the computer screen. Now you could even see what you were doing before the page was printed. From tape-driven repetitive typing to today's computer-driven text manipulation was a mere blip on the office products time line.

As PCs began to be more readily available for business use, the huge old command-driven "hard-wired" word processors, with the programs built right into the systems, began to die out.[2] The built-in software in machines like the IBM System 6, Exxon's Vydec and the Dictaphone 3000 eventually was replaced with very expensive tiny software programs with a fraction of the function of the old dinosaurs.

---

2 The Dictaphone 3000 had a "mnemonic keyboard" with 92
   combination keyboard commands that ran the program. An
   entire new discipline grew up around such horrors—ergonomics.

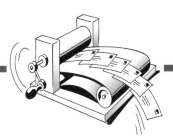

Now we've come full circle: As we've said before, machines are getting smaller (notebook size and even "palm-tops") and software is getting more and more complex, like the giant systems that started the whole thing.

Briefumschlaugverarbeitung

Before we move on, let's talk about envelopes for a minute, probably the most essential yet the most exasperating job in the computerized office. Are you still producing your envelopes on your typewriter? You are not alone.

Once upon a time there was a wondrous machine called the IBM System 6, an all-in-one "console" text processor/printer combination. It was a high-volume production machine, the best paper handler in the office products business. It could produce a letter and envelope, collated, in three minutes flat (greased lightning by WP standards in those days). It had a kind of Rube Goldberg personality as it busied itself doing what was called *merge-file-text,* but with its "state-of-the-art" built-in inkjet printer, it did a very good job.

It wasn't perfect. Typists repaired to the restroom in tears after trying to read the manual, and the console was as big as several typical office cubicles.

When the "6" went away, nothing as good ever replaced it. At last, heavy-duty WP software programs and office printers are catching up, having finally conquered the "one-off" envelope. (To do more, you need a printer with an envelope feeder—kind of like a System 6.) See *One-Off Envelopes and Labels* in this chapter for how envelopes are done today.

One-Offs to Small Batches

All PC application programs can capture and record information, call it back, change it and print it. Furthermore, virtually all word processors can spellcheck, format, auto-replace and use typographic fonts. If this is still news to you, you should probably take the "Short Course in Personal Computing" in the *Reference* before you go on.

In this section, you'll see how word processors speed the production of documents by recycling what you've already done.

Machines are invented to do repetitive work so people can spend their time doing something that takes brains. However, just as some people persist in using their computers as glorified typewriters, others use them as clumsy duplicating devices—one page at a time.

> ***au·to·ma·tion*** *n.* 1: *The technique of making an apparatus, a process or a system operate automatically.*

Hold the Macros

Before you panic, let's set your expectations.

The advances made in word processing in recent years are pretty scary. Today, you're supposed to go from simple typing to quasi-programming routines that fine-tune your output ("*if* balance is greater than $1000, *then* send the nasty letter; *else* send the nice one").

Or on a lesser plane, you're expected to know how to write little macros (keystroke recording routines) to create those letters or memos with the

built-in prompts that stop at the blanks and won't let the typist pass until every blank is filled in.

This book deals with simpler matters. Most of the people we know who are trying to develop a business or an organization have no time to learn sophisticated programming techniques. So let's concentrate on the basics. By the time your office is turning out 300 letters and envelopes in an afternoon, you'll be ready to learn more on your own.

One-Offs

When you're finally pleased with your letter-perfect introductory document, why not just call it back, change a couple of words, re-address it, save it to a new name and send it out again? We all do it and it works just fine for one or two letters at a time, with reasonable care. Long before computers, an overworked typist with a steady hand at the paper cutter, a fresh supply of letterhead, a good copier and a myopic boss could accomplish the same thing.

So what's wrong with it? The temptation is to keep right on copying and tweaking for four, five or a dozen or more letters, and before you know it one error is multiplied by two, then three, then four. An easy-to-achieve blooper is to forget to change the document name and save your new letter over the old one, erasing any record of what went to the first person. (This is the moment you discover a typo in the original letter.)

That kind of recycling eventually gets you into trouble. All it takes is one stupendous gaffe to cure you of the practice forever. You know the drill: You write a great letter to your best customer. Then you clone it for your next best customer, a permanent enemy of the first, but you forget to expunge client #1's product name from the body of the letter. Say good-bye to your credibility.

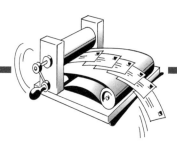

> **Errata.** *"It is estimated that 5% of all [business] letters
> written are to correct errors or omissions."*
> —The Secretary's Handbook, 10th Edition.

So if you're wise, you'll limit the recycling of one-offs to a very careful few.

One-Off Envelopes and Labels

Having produced the letter, you need a matching envelope. This is how modern word processors have finally solved the envelope problem, and truth to tell, it's simpler than the System 6.

1. Open your one-off letter and highlight just the inside address. Be sure to include the name and ZIP Code, but don't include any extra paragraph marks before the text block.

2. Choose the envelope command.

    For example, it's on the Layout menu in WordPerfect and in Microsoft Word for Windows it's an icon on the menu bar or a command on the Tools menu. It's worth searching for this command.

3. Once you've entered the envelope command, explore the options offered for other useful functions like *print return address* or *include USPS POSTNET* or *FIM* (barcodes).

    See *Delivery* or the *Glossary* for more on these USPS terms.

4. Put an envelope in the printer and choose the print command.

If you have problems, the printer options might have to be set for manual feed or you might have to change the paper orientation to the way your printer feeds envelopes.

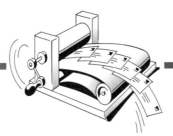

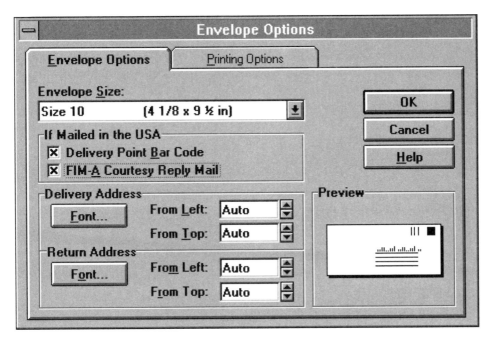

Envelopes & Labels Dialog Box

If you asked for one, the system generates a barcode based on the ZIP Code in the address. (Make sure the ZIP you type is correct!)

> **Smart Mailer's Tip.** *If you type the ZIP+4 in the address, at least one word processor gives you the full delivery point barcode. In the* Delivery *chapter, you'll see how important this can be.*

To produce one-off labels, use the same process. The Labels command is on the Layout menu in WordPerfect and on the Tools menu in Word for Windows.

Small Batch Processing

You can get even more mileage out of that perfect letter, so spend all the time you need to get it right. The payback in typing, proofreading and correction is enormous.

The two principal ways to move from one-offs to small batches of letters without compromising quality are shell letters and boilerplate. All word processors can do these things; unfortunately, they all call them different names. If you persevere you can find something close to these techniques in your manual or in Help.

Be sure to save a copy of your letter before you start experimenting with small batches.

The Shell Game

Most robust text editing programs offer some means of creating original custom shell documents from your own perfected letter, memo or other communiqué. Your program may call the shell document a template, stationery or some other special name to distinguish it from a standard document. The shell is not to be confused with forms or merge letters that are coded to prompt for fill-ins. The shell letter is much more basic.

Shell letters are the easiest way to speed production of letters that need very little customizing. By storing the document as a template, you're assured the format, styles and text won't be altered accidentally. Every document will be Letter Perfect.

The shell is stored as a special filetype (SALESLET.DOT in Word, SALESLET.WPT in WordPerfect, for example).

Here are the generic steps for creating a shell:

1. Perfect your letter; spellcheck and proofread it carefully.

   Delete the date, inside address and salutation name.
   (Leave the word "Dear" and the colon.)

2. Choose Save As and check a box or change the filetype to save it as a shell.

   MacWrite Pro calls the filetype for a shell letter Stationery; Word for Windows calls it a Document Template, and WordPerfect refers to the Template Document. (The WordPerfect preformatted templates are called ExpressDocs.)

3. Click OK or press Enter.

To use your custom shell:

1. Open a *new* document.

   Choose your custom template as the document style or type. A copy of the master is copied to the screen. As a safety measure, save it to a new name with a regular document filetype right away.

2. Type the date, inside address and salutation name.

3. Proofread those parts carefully.

4. Save the finished letter again.

5. Print it, sign it and send it.

6. Use the one-off technique to print an envelope.

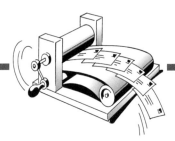

Boilerplate

In an effort to differentiate their products, word processing publishers have all but obscured another easy form of semi-automation, boilerplate. (The word implies something indestructible, protective.) The whole point of boilerplate is to *prevent* editing to reduce the opportunity for introducing errors.

The legal profession has made an art of paragraph assembly, as it is sometimes called. The same principle can be applied to your business documents. (Let's hope yours are more interesting than legal boilerplate.)

Let's use the Great American Swiss Army Machine to make canned paragraphs from your letter:

1. Call up your perfect letter.

2. Highlight paragraph 1, your knock-'em-dead opener.

3. Give the command to save it as a boilerplate paragraph.

    In Word for Windows, boilerplate is handled as AutoText. In WordPerfect, Abbreviations does about the same thing. MacWrite Pro and other word processors for the Mac (System 7.0 and up) use a feature called Publish and Subscribe to save and use boilerplate. DOS WP programs may refer to Glossary or yet another term. Keep looking—it's worth finding this feature.

4. Give this paragraph a name.

    Write it down. Many programs allot only one to three characters for the boilerplate designator, so it will take some effort to devise a naming scheme that's easy to remember.

5. Repeat for each reusable paragraph.

Boilerplate is by no means foolproof. In a custom template the amount of variable information can be carefully controlled, but when you assemble

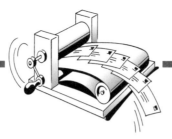

a patchwork document you have to make decisions about the order and relevance of the content. If you have a large collection, it isn't too difficult to make really silly errors.

Don't skip the planning stage even for semi-automated letters. You may have to edit your paragraphs to make sure each can stand alone. Keep a log of the paragraphs and group them by category. You could start several series of paragraphs for different kinds of customers. Be sure to save your standard closing and signature block as a separate entry. Save a printout of the paragraphs for reference. Save and close the boilerplate document.

Now when you write to prospective clients, you have tested copy that works: a bit about your company (Intro-1), several paragraphs about your technical capabilities (Tech-1, Tech-2) or marketing expertise (Mkt-1, Mkt-2) and your standard closer. You can mix and match the paragraphs to suit each reader.

Here's how to assemble a boilerplate letter:

1. Open a new file.

2. Type the date and inside address.

3. Call up each paragraph that's appropriate for this individual.

4. Save the letter under a new name.

5. Print it, sign it and mail it.

Boilerplate and custom shells are wonderful tools especially for small mailings where you can spend a little more time customizing each letter.

Now you've taken your mailing projects from a single one-off letter and envelope to multiple letters with several degrees of semi-automation. It's time to get serious about accelerating your outreach program—and set up your system once so your computer can do most of the work.

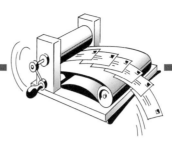

Mass Appeal

Good customers can't be replaced, yet some managers take for granted their most valuable business asset, their contacts. Look through your correspondence files, telephone lists and card files for important clues about your business: Who calls about what? Who pays on time? Who buys regularly? These facts should be carefully preserved in one special place—your Master Contacts List. This list is central to your business. Fill it with accurate information about your customers and prospects, keep it up to date, and safeguard it with your life against fire, theft or natural disaster! It isn't overcautious to store a copy of this list off site.

The PC is the perfect tool for collecting contact information and saving it in electronic database files that are easy to use and easy to change. Eventually, you'll merge your database with your perfect letter, suitably coded, to turn out hundreds of letters without your help. Your productivity will take a giant step forward, limited only by the speed and capacity of your printer.

When you merge selected records from your lists with word-processed letters, you don't have to rekey that critical address information. If the database is correct, the inside addresses and the envelopes will be correct.

The Database

Just as word processors share common capabilities, database or list management programs have a family resemblance. Some are more sophisticated than others and may give you more features than you'll ever use.

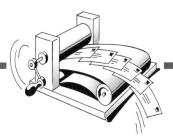

You want your database program to:

- Store the separate parts of a name and address.

- Sort on any part that makes sense—last name, ZIP, city, state and so on.

- Let you select partial lists by common characteristics—all vice presidents of purchasing might be a good target.

- Give you space for keeping notes about each person.

- Print formatted layouts of your name and address file.

- Work together with your word processor's shell letters, envelopes and labels to handle the mail production operation for you.

Picture your card file neatly sorted, with no unsightly corrections and with a pointer that instantly finds any contact by name, company or even hobby. That's a database.

If you think ahead, your database can give you the records for every customer with past due invoices, or every prospect in New York State, or every client in the insurance industry. That's something your card file can't do. The trick is in the database design.

Build your Master Contacts List with your word processor's built-in list program, or with a more robust program such as FileMaker Pro, Microsoft Access, dBase, FoxPro or any of the popular database programs.

> **WP Meets DB.** *Check to see which database programs your word processor can use. One of the many flavors of .DBF usually works. Some word processors can even interact with a spreadsheet or table file as the data source.*

Some programs offer more advanced functions that work with other programs such as your mainframe financial system.

Before you start building, think about how you want to use your list. The whole point of a database is to make automated information processing possible—to perform the same operation on more than one record without human intervention. With careful planning, what you can do with one name and address you can do with every name and address on your list in one process.

If you start off right, you can make sure every list you set up is structured the same way.

Planning

It will help you plan your list if you understand the basic makeup of the most common databases. A database is a *file* of information made up of individual *records* containing separate *fields* of data. Even though terminology and structures are changing—you're likely to read about *tables* and *field properties* these days—the essential information doesn't change all that much. The common element is the field, the smallest item of data in the file.

MASTER RECORD FIELD NAMES	TITLE	FIRSTNAME	LASTNAME	SALUTATION
RECORD 1	MR.	MICHAEL	ANGELO	MIKE
RECORD 2	DR.	ABEL	BAKER	ABE
RECORD 3	LIEUT.	CHARLES	DAVID	CHARLIE

Elements of a database

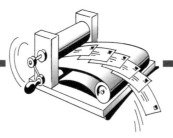

Jot down all the ways you might want to use your contact information: letters, invoices, envelopes, electronic address book, or maybe a telephone or fax list. This will help you determine how many fields you need for every record.

You should consider at least seven main information categories for business targets.

- Name
- Business affiliation
- Street Address (with mail stop)
- Town
- State
- ZIP Code (ZIP+4 is recommended)
- Contact numbers

Most businesses break their lists down even further into subcategories for their own purposes, and add a memo field to keep notes about the contact.

Consider again the name information. Will you always start your letters Dear Mr. Prospect, or would you sometimes write Dear Harry? Is Harry a doctor?

Here's a good way to store Name information:

- Last name
- Suffix (Jr., Esq.)
- Middle initial
- First name
- Honorific (Dr., Mr., Ms.)
- Salutation (Dear "?"—Harry? Mr. Jones?)

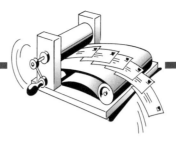

For maximum flexibility separate the business affiliation data like this:

■ Title

■ Company name

■ Department

■ Industry

The Industry field makes it possible to segment your market and send a special announcement to top human resources executives in the chemical industry, or production managers in the automotive industry, or marketing vice presidents in telecommunications. You don't need a complex conditional programming statement to target a special group. Just select the records you want from the whole database first and save them as a subset.

Put the number and street together in one field, but a post office box should be in a separate field. You'll see why in the *Delivery* chapter.

Add special fields for your own purposes, such as a code to give each name a marketing priority. (It would be a pity to waste your ten-dollar brochure on the wrong target.)

The Postal Service needs at least this information for a business address:

>   *Company name*
>   *Street address or P.O. Box*
>   *Town*
>   *State*
>   *ZIP Code*

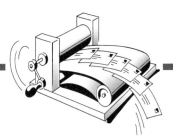

Town, state and ZIP are key fields for sorting to take advantage of postal discounts and faster delivery. The more detailed the ZIP, the faster the mail gets to its destination. See *SmartMail* in the next chapter for more on ZIP Codes.

Make as many telephone number fields as you think you'll use. A telephone number, extension, FAX number and even a home number might be important to you. For a sales information database, you can't have too many ways to get in touch.

Building

Virtually any electronic database is built the same way. First you tell the software you're starting a new file or table. Then you name the master fields to match your design. You describe each master field by the type of data it will contain. (Like word processors, many database programs offer templates of commonly used field names.)

Once you've defined all the fields, they're saved as the master record. Then you use the master record as a template, filling in the information for every name and address on your list.

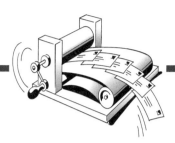

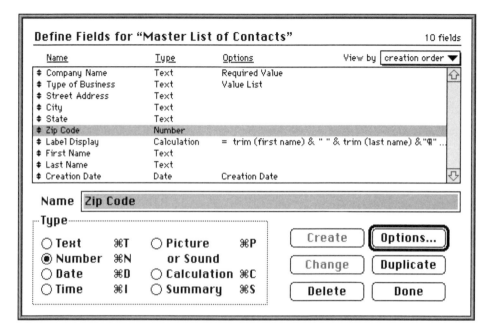

FileMaker Pro master record with fields named and defined
—Courtesy of Claris Corporation

The data pulled from individual records in the database are called *variables* because they vary from record to record. For example, the CITY field might be filled in with Chicago, Philadelphia or New York, depending on which record the computer is reading. As you save a completed record, a new blank one takes its place. If you enter the data carefully, you only have to do it once until the information changes.

> **Check and Double-Check.** *If your database program has a spellchecker, use it. If it doesn't, proofread on screen and on a printout before you use the mailing list.*

Set up a regular routine for making changes to your list as you receive address changes or other information. A clean list is even more important than a useful database structure.

> **Clean your List.** *A list is only as good as it is deliverable.*

Plan your master fields off line. Write down each field name with an estimate of the length required for the longest entry. For example, a LASTNAME field with only five characters will work for Jones and Smith, but Thompson won't fit. Now follow these steps on line to create the master fields:

1. Open a new file.

2. Choose the option to make a new database.

3. Define the first master field (like the title or first name).

4. Enter the number of characters for the field.

5. Enter the field type (character, number, date or other).

> **Alpha and Numeric.** *Alphabetic fields are really alphanumeric. They can even be all numbers, as long as the numbers are not used in calculations. For example, the ZIP field should be designated as alphanumeric in some programs to prevent the numbers from being added or multiplied, or the hyphen (if it's part of the entry) from acting as a subtraction operator.*
>
> *Most programs let you define numeric fields down to the number of decimals or format (dollar sign, commas and so on).*

6. Enter any other rules for the data in this field.

   For example, is this field required or optional? (That is, can you leave it blank when entering data?) Add any other special properties as part of your field definition.

7. Repeat for every field in the master record.

8. Check the master record carefully before saving it.

Once all the master fields are defined, you add the data records, the names and addresses from your card files and file folders. If your structure doesn't work for all the entries, you can stop adding records and modify the master record to make the fields the right size.

Before you start adding records, though, decide which way to spell company names and common abbreviations. Make sure your entries are uniform. For example, if you have several entries for General Electric, either use the full name or GE but not both. You want the computer to find all the company records when it does a search.

1. Choose the command to add records.

   In Microsoft Access, you Add Records to a Form or Datasheet associated with the table. In FoxPro, you Append Records. A blank record showing all the defined fields is presented.

2. Fill in each field in the blank record, tabbing from field to field.

   The rules for each field are already defined, so you couldn't enter a name in a date field, for example, even if you wanted to.

3. Press ENTER when you've filled in all the fields.

   The next blank record pops up (or you're asked if you want to continue adding records).

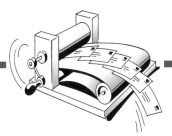

4. Continue until all the records have been entered.

5. Tell the system you're finished. Save the file and close it.

A quick way to build your database is to import an existing list, such as appropriate data from your spreadsheet program.

You can use this database to print reports showing the status of your accounts, or sales activity or other custom reports of your own design. Basically you tell the system which fields you want to have printed where.

> ***Save Me.*** *Some DB programs don't have a Save command. The system does its own housekeeping and saves automatically. But look before you Close. If there is a Save, use it!*

The Rented List

You can rent lists of just about every demographic description. Many of them are highly reliable, and if you're starting from scratch to send upwards of 5,000-10,000 pieces at one time, a rented list may be a good idea.

Most marketers agree, though, that the best list is the one you build yourself from your own customers and contacts.

Whether you build or buy, if you're doing large mailings, look into a list management software tool to help validate your database. (See the special section in the *Reference* for more about list management software.)

Market Analysis Tools: Add value to your list by subscribing to a demographic market analysis program. Some come with large standardized market information databases on CDs. These tools can be used to compare your list to

scientifically segmented markets that reveal the populations' buying habits, lifestyles, education, income, occupation and other interesting data.

Checklist for Database Management

✔ Establish a standard way to enter the field data for name and address records.

✔ Use standard postal abbreviations for the parts of an address and other data.

✔ Clean your list frequently.

✔ Maintain your list in any convenient order—account number, alphabetical by company or last name—but before you mail, sort first by company and secondarily by last name to eliminate the duplicates.

✔ For large mailings, sort by ZIP Code before you merge and print.

✔ Establish an office routine for making database updates.

✔ Maintain a hard copy of your database.

✔ Keep a backup file of your database off premises in case of disaster.

The Merge

Now it all comes together in your genuine, automated, PC-generated, business mail factory. You need two files for your production number: the Master Contacts List and the shell letter, which you'll modify in a minute.

Your WP program has its own name for these files and the process for putting them together. In WordPerfect for Windows, the terms are *Form File* for the shell and *Data File* for the list. The process is called *Merge*. Word for

Windows calls the files the *Main Document* and *Data Source,* and their marriage is *Mail Merge.* Both systems start from the Tools menu. MacWrite Pro calls it *Mail Merge* too, but you work with a *Data Document* and *Form Letter* and you start at the File menu.

Your PC, printer, database and word processing program will do all the work and turn out finished product at a rate of six to twelve pieces a minute. (Try *that* on your typewriter!) And you'll be amazed at how fast the post office is going to whip these letters through the system once you learn how to address them correctly, in the next chapter.

The Merge Document

One last recycling of your perfect letter will complete your journey through the stages of automation. This time, where you took out the inside address, you'll put in the codes, or master record field names, that tell the computer the data to insert in each letter to personalize it. You can make this pretty complicated by adding macros or conditional statements, but for first-time automation (and until you are comfortable with the concepts), keep it simple. Make another copy of your letter before you start making it into a merge document.

Here's what you do (the order may be different for your word processor):

1. Open the shell letter.

2. Choose the Merge command from the Tools or File menu.

3. Identify your shell as the form to use.

4. Identify your Master Contacts List as the list or data file to use.

    Now the system knows which database's fields it should search.

<<Date>>

<<Honorific>> <<First>> <<Last>>
<<Title>>
<<Company>>
<<Delivery Address>>
<<City>>, <<State>> <<ZIP>>

Dear <<Salutation>>:

This is to remind you…body text body text body text body text body text body text body text body text body text body text.

We'd like to help you out but you've owed us <<balance>> since…body text body text body text body text body text body text. Body text body text body text. Body text body text body text today.

Sincerely yours,

Signature

Typed signature
Title

enc: list of enclosures

The Shell Letter with Field Codes

5. With the cursor in the position for the inside address, choose the command to insert field codes.

Usually you click a button with a pretty obvious label such as Insert Field (WordPerfect) or Insert Merge Field (Word). The field name pops into the document with special formatting to set it off from the standard text.

6. Type the punctuation or spacing required between the field codes.

For example, put the colon after the field code for <<salutation>>. Otherwise, every salutation field would have to contain the colon as well as the name.

7. Proofread and save the document.

The important thing to remember is the list file and the main document both have to be open when you insert the codes and while the merge takes place. Here are the generic steps for merging the data file with your main document:

1. Turn the printer on and load the letterhead, envelope, postcard or other shell form.

2. Open the coded document.

3. Identify the database and "attach" it to the main document.

> ***About that Database.*** *Remember, you can use a subset rather than the whole thing: all the Vice Presidents of Marketing, all the past due accounts....*

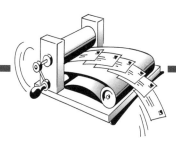

September 1, 1996

Mr. Michael Angelo
Vice President, Facilities
Sistine Systems, Inc.
P.O. Box 1110
Rome, New York 13440-1110

Dear Mike:

This is to remind you...body text body text body text body text body text body text body text body text body text body text.

We'd like to help you out but you've owed us $5,507.50 since body text body text body text body text body text body text. Body text body text body text. Body text body text body text today.

Sincerely yours,

Signature

Typed signature
Title

enc: list of enclosures

One Merged Letter

4. Choose the command for merging.

   When you give the signal to start the merge, the system searches the database for fields that match the codes. When it finds a match, it copies the information in the database field into the document.

5. Send the resulting customized documents to the printer or to a file to be printed later.

That's a vastly simplified look at merging variable data with constant text. Once you master this basic merge technique, read up on fine-tuning your output in your user guide. Most word processors offer advanced techniques such as conditional clauses (IF *this field is blank*/THEN *close up the space*/ELSE *print as usual*.)

> ***Testing...Testing.*** *Once your files are ready, you can merge them straight to the printer or (for small batches) play it safe and send the results to a file so you can check the letters before you use good stationery.*
>
> *Whatever you do, test the merge on a small number of records first to make sure the data pop into the right fields.*

Your system can personalize and automate any of the letters, postcards, envelopes, brochures, mailers, reply devices—any document you can make that your printer can print.

Key Points for Mail Merge

Here are some quick tips about mail merge:

- Be sure the field code names you put in the main document are identical to the master record field names in the database.

- If you put a field code in the body of the letter, make sure all records you're merging have relevant data in that field or the sentence may not make sense in the merged letter. Example:

> *We'd like to help you out but you've owed us **oil paint** since...*

- A quick way to verify your shell letter field codes is to put just the codes in a separate document and merge them with the database. The bad data will jump out at you. Example:

<<Name>>	*<<Address>>*	*<<Salutation>>:*	*<<balance>>*
.	.	*Mike*	*oil paint*
.	.	*Abe*	*$5,507.50*
.	.	*Charlie*	*$3,300,030.30*
.	.	*90029-5555*	*Vincent*

- The last thing you do before merging a document with 500 records is ***proofread!*** Remember, every time you touch a document you have a chance to make a mistake.

Producing the Desktop Marketing Kit

So now you've sent out an introductory letter to a very long list. Are you ready to send more information when you get all those responses? That's where your desktop marketing kit comes in.

An Inside Job

Printing in house may not be the wisest choice or even the least expensive. What are the considerations for keeping the job inside or sending it out?

One of the chief attractions to completing the production cycle in house is control. You have all the tools you need for most jobs; you keep your proprietary list safe from outsiders; you alone are responsible for costs— no surprises.

Another is convenience. If something goes wrong, you're right there to fix it. You can check the proofs without leaving your office. Run your print job after hours when no one else needs the printer.

Cost can be a determining factor. Printing in house means printing exactly what you need when you need it. (It's been called on-demand printing.) You won't have to take that 10% overrun whether you want it or not, a printing trade custom.

A compelling reason to keep your printing in house is change. Is yours a new enterprise, still feeling its way and finding its voice? You'll love being able to make changes and turn around a new mailing in days rather than weeks.

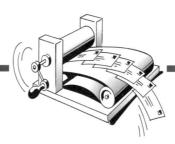

Going Outside

For your database marketing, if you send more than 300 to 500 mail merge letters a week, you might consider a service bureau. Most of them can accept your database and merge documents by modem. Here are some tips for using a service bureau:

- Make sure you choose a reliable service bureau if you value your proprietary list. Get references from companies like yours before you turn over your files.

- Keep an exact copy of the files you've turned over so you can back up any claims if there are any problems at the bureau end.

- "Salt" your database file so you can monitor its use. Salting means entering a number of records in the list that will come back to you.

For your direct marketing kit, before you even think about commercial printers, buy these two books: *Pocket Pal* by International Paper Company and *Getting it Printed* from Coast-to-Coast Printing.

Since its first printing in 1934, *Pocket Pal* has held the hands of countless novices as they venture into the world of commercial printing. It introduces terminology and printing concepts that will help you hold your own when you're talking with your printer.

Getting it Printed gives valuable information about each step of the production process from writing print specs to binding options. We won't duplicate that information here. Instead, we'll point out some things to consider in going to an outside printer.

Almost every kind of business mail you examined in the *Design* and *Desktop Marketing* chapters can be produced on a standard desktop laser or inkjet printer. However, unless you have a special tray for 11 x 17 paper you will have to go outside to print a brochure with a fold size of 8½ x 11 inches.

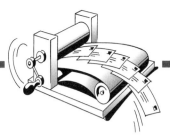

You may also have to produce the reply device, a postcard, outside if your office printer can't handle index-weight card stock easily.

> ***Jam Session.*** *Don't try to produce two-sided printing in large quantities, especially on heavy stock, unless you have a duplex printer. Feeding the paper through twice is a labor-intensive, accident-prone process.*

If you have a duplex printer and are printing your mailer in house, liven things up with the special papers like the ones shown in *Desktop Marketing*.

Even the pages you can't print in house can be taken at least as far as camera-ready copy (CRC) before you go outside.

Desktop Publishing a Mailer

This is a typical sequence for developing a mailer with your desktop publishing program:

1. Choose a one-page, tri-fold brochure template.

   The templates may be available from the File menu or in another special menu. A copy of the template is displayed, perhaps filled in with dummy text (called greeking) and picture placeholders.

2. Replace the greeked text with your own.

   Type the copy directly in the page comp program, or better, place or import a file you've already typed and proofed.

3. Arrange the new text throughout the template.

   As you manipulate the text, it will flow around the picture placeholders.

4. Apply the template's styles to the headings and other text elements.

5. Select a picture placeholder and give the command to import or place your own graphic file in its place.

   Use freehand drawings created with a graphics software program, or scans of photographs and artwork. Make sure the artwork is original or used with permission. (Check to be sure there are no restrictions on using your clip art.)

6. Adjust the text and pictures and amend the styles to suit your taste.

For an inexpensive, low-resolution, one-color outside print job:

1. Print one set of pages on regular paper.

2. Load special prepress paper in your printer.

3. Print each page on a separate sheet.

4. Print thumbnails to show the correct orientation of the pages.

5. Paste the draft pages together in the correct orientation and fold them correctly.

The printer might make paper printing plates directly from your laser output for a low-cost job. Remember, what you see is what you're going to get, so take a close look at the graphics, particularly, and decide if they look good enough on your master copy. If they don't, mark the pictures on the masters FPO, meaning For Position Only. Send along the electronic files or the original pictures for the printer to handle.

It's wise to pay a little more and have the printer fold the mailer for you. The automatic equipment gives a sharper look than hand-folding can achieve. For heavy stock, the printer may have to score the piece before folding.

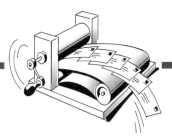

To get higher resolution (finer, sharper print) at low cost:

1. Ask your printer what kind of electronic files are needed to make film.

2. Print the job to a file such as .EPS (Encapsulated PostScript).

   In the print setup dialog box, check the option that specifies that the output contains all the files needed for remote printing. That will pick up all linked pictures and other files.

3. If you supply copy on disk, make sure the prepress people have the fonts they need or supply fonts with your file.

Until you know enough about printing, leave the more complicated jobs to your prepress service bureau. You'll learn a lot.

Key Points for Outside Printing

■ Not every printer can do every kind of job. Reputable printers will tell you what their equipment does best and whether or not your job is appropriate for their shop. (The *Pocket Pal* can help here.)

■ A large, long-run production facility may be more expensive on a short-run job than a smaller print shop. It's all in the equipment. What size page can the press accommodate?

■ Get more than one bid for all but the smallest jobs. Prepare detailed written print specifications so bids can be compared. Evaluate the bids on 1) specific responses to your requirements, 2) price and 3) schedule.

■ Responsiveness is the most important. Does the printer understand what you want? Will there be hidden charges for things you or the printer omitted? A good printer will ask questions before bidding and point out problem areas in your Request for Quote (RFQ). This is how you get your education about print production.

- Make a study of paper, often the greatest cost in a print job. Surprisingly, recycled paper can be more costly than new paper. Always get a sample of the paper to be used on your job and compare it to the final product.

  If your printer suggests a different paper, listen. Print shops usually stock "house" papers in quantity. You can save money if the house paper is appropriate for your job.

- When you hand off a job to a printer, keep a photocopy of your mechanical. The mechanical is your camera-ready copy (CRC). Keep an exact copy of that file untouched in a safe place until the job is over.

- Deliver a dummy or mockup of the final product with the mechanical. Keep an exact copy of the dummy for yourself. Any faulty pagination or other assembly errors can be traced to the source and corrected at no cost to you if your mockup was correct.

- Get proofs (bluelines) of the negatives, the film from which the printing plates are made. Check them over very carefully with a jeweler's loupe or magnifying glass. Look for broken type, uneven density, smudges, specks, dings and other flaws. Mark any flaws right on the bluelines and make sure they are corrected. If there are a lot of flaws, ask for a second set of proofs.

- A tiny speck can look like a boulder on the final copy. On the other hand, there is no such thing as paper without some natural flaws.

Color is an entire book in itself. One reason to use outside printers is their expertise in printing color. Your little four-color inkjet is not up to a major run of brochures. Here are some things you have to do to get good color:

- Ask your art director or graphic designer to help with quality control on a color job.

- Have the mechanical prepared with a tissue overlay that shows all the color breaks. Check it very carefully.

- To keep costs down, use color wisely. If the colors don't touch other elements, color separations usually won't be required. If you don't "bleed" the color off the page, you might be able to use a smaller press.

- You can get a multicolor look without the cost by specifying tints (percentages of color or black) to accent certain areas.

- Provide a swatch of the color you require. Color swatches, just like paint chips, are available for many color matching systems.

- Ask for color proofs rather than bluelines; that is, overlay proofs or integral color proofs. The overlays show the color breaks but don't do a very good job on matching color. Integrals or match prints are the closest you'll get to the real thing.

- For complex multicolor jobs, do a press check. That means examining the actual sheets as they come off the press. Check every detail for correct color registration. Don't be afraid to ask for more press sheets until you see one that meets your standards. You won't get a second chance. Initial each press sheet you approve and make sure the final product matches it.

You've gone from one-offs to batches to mass production in one short chapter.

Now you have to get your output delivered. Read on.

Delivery

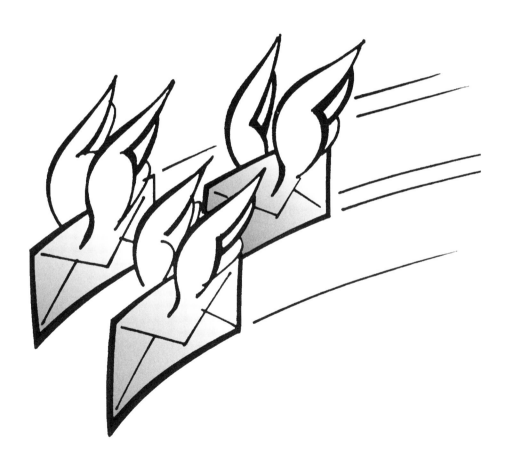

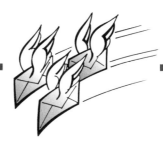

Delivery

Now that you're producing Big Mail, what can you do to help it on its way to your customers? And how can you reduce the number of pieces that miss their mark?

During an interview for this book, a Postal Service representative made this wry comment: *"If your mail has an address and postage on it, we'll deliver it. Where and how soon is up to you."*

This chapter demystifies the automated mailing system and puts you in charge of your mailing operation. You'll learn how to address your mail so it won't get lost in the vast complexities of the postal system. Delivery is all about:

- Taking control and Managing Your Mail

- Creating Smart Mail for faster, more efficient delivery

- Preparing for Big Mail

But before you dive into the world of ZIP Codes, barcodes and optical character readers, look back for a moment at the beginnings of automated mail.

Making History

The U.S. Postal Service and Pitney Bowes have been business partners for many years. In fact, the USPS is probably responsible for bringing together that well-known team of Mr. Pitney and Mr. Bowes. *It all goes back more than 90 years…*

POSTOFFICE RAID YIELDS $74,610 TO BURGLARS.

Wholesale Stamp Vault Is Entered
by Tunnel and Swept Practically Clean.

STEEL FLOOR IS PIERCED.

Suspicious horse and light express wagon at scene.

FEW CLEWS LEFT BEHIND.

These headlines from *The Chicago Daily Tribune,* October, 1901, started a chain of events that set Mr. Pitney on a path that would inevitably converge with the road traveled by Mr. Bowes. No, Mr. Pitney didn't steal the stamps, but that robbery gave his invention the endorsement it needed to gain wider acceptance.

Mr. Pitney...

In his own words, *"The idea of a Postage Meter first occurred to Mr. A. H. Pitney in 1901, while connected with a Mail Order Wall Paper house of Chicago, as a result of his observations of the ease with which the office boys could, and did, appropriate the money entrusted to them for the purchase of postage stamps."*[1]

1 From the Pitney Bowes archives

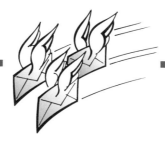

Pitney's simple, sturdy machine was a hand-powered plunger device with counters for tallying the imprints that represented an amount of prepaid postage. A locking mechanism shut down the machine when the amount paid for was exhausted.

The invention did not impress the Postmaster of Chicago, F. E. Coyne, who thought the idea of replacing the traditional postage stamp was *"too absurd to merit very much consideration."*

In October of that same year, Coyne changed his tune when those famous horse-and-buggy thieves cleaned out his vault. It took a special Act of Congress to relieve Mr. Coyne of the burden of repaying the money. Suddenly Mr. Pitney's idea looked a lot better.

Mr. Pitney organized the Pitney Postal Machine Company and continued to improve the design. The company built a larger, rotary-type test model and shipped it to Postmaster General Payne in Washington, DC where it was reviewed more favorably by a Special Committee.

Unfortunately, the Attorney General of the United States decided that special legislation would be required before this imprint could be allowed to replace the stamp.

Three Postmaster Generals later, the first official test of the new machine was authorized and took place at the National Tribune Company in Washington in May of 1912. The tests were successful, but the machine still met resistance from the bureaucrats. The Third Assistant Postmaster General said, in 1914, *"while the tests demonstrate that the machine is not without mechanical merit…there is no need of such a machine as an adjunct to the Postal Service."*

Mr. Pitney eventually became a stockbroker.

"MACHINE TO STOP STAMP LOSSES"—Technical World, February, 1914

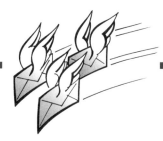

...Meet Mr. Bowes.

Meanwhile, Mr. W. H. Bowes, President of the Universal Stamping Machine Company of Stamford, Connecticut—government contractors for canceling machines—was developing a plan for expediting First-Class Mail preparation (and not so coincidentally, expanding the market for his products). At that time, the Permit System allowed only bulk mailings of identical third-class pieces to carry a permit imprint. The customer paid for the postage at the counter. Mr. Bowes' plan, "The Bowes Mailing System," was submitted on September 13, 1918.

> ***Mr. Bowes' Plan.*** *"First, the extension of the Permit System to First-Class Mail. Second, the approval by the Department of the use in the offices of large mailers of machines similar to Post Office cancelling machines, these machines to be equipped with counting registers directly geared to the printing member so as to insure an accurate count by each imprint; the register to be sealed and locked by the Postmaster and subject to their [sic] inspection at all times."*

His plan was rejected because it *"did not safeguard the Postal Revenues and would tend to increase...the work in the Post Office."* There was sufficient interest in a meter that *did* safeguard revenues and reduce the workload, however, to lead Mr. Bowes to encourage Mr. Pitney to leave the stocks and bonds business to help design the new machine.

The Pitney-Bowes Postage Meter Company was born.

The Pitney-Bowes Model "A" Machine—circa 1920

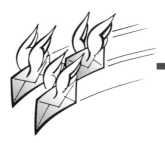

Managing Your Mail

Rule number one for high-impact business mail is: Schedule it. Random business mail generates random responses, if any—nothing you could measure or predict.

As you read earlier, each piece you send is part of the overall impression you make on your customers and prospects. A hit-or-miss approach misses the mark entirely: The cumulative effect of your business mail is far greater than the impact of any individual piece.

The mail that gets noticed and read has a steady, purposeful, we're-going-to-be-around-for-a-while feel to it. Each new piece brings to mind other pieces you have sent. To get that cumulative, purposeful effect, you need a plan.

Plan It

Just as you outline the content of each piece and plan the structure of your list, you can outline your mailing strategy on a yearly calendar. Decide what you can afford to send and how often to keep in touch with at least your current customers. Mail forwarding (free for First-Class Mail) expires after one year.

> **Keeping Current.** *Some mailing experts recommend sending mail to your list at least four times a year to keep it fresh and responsive. More often might be better: The National Address Information Center in Memphis sends master file updates to its agencies every two weeks!*

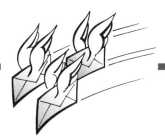

Aim It

In an informal study for this book, we asked some questions of people in corporations using Word for Windows 6.0 for repetitive departmental correspondence. Two questions in particular drew interesting responses:

Q: How many pieces of mail do you send per mailing?

A: Answers ranged from 25 to 1400, weekly and monthly.

Q: How do you rate your knowledge of USPS requirements for correct addressing?

A: 88.9% answered *zero.*

The mail may be getting to the post office sooner, but what then?

Progress Report

In the 1850s, it took several months to deliver a letter to California by overland stagecoach or boat. Today, *Postally Correct* First-Class Mail is delivered anywhere in the U.S., including Hawaii, in two to three days. (You can't count the time your letter lingers in the mail room.)

The Postal Service has worked hard to keep up with our increasing numbers and native reluctance to stay in one place very long. Traditionally the USPS subsidizes and participates in the development of new technologies, and over the years has pioneered the use of new modes of transportation to reach us wherever we are.

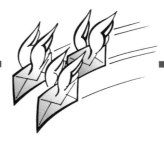

O, Pioneers. [2]

Navigable waters declared "post roads"	*– 1823*
Short-run steam trains carry the mail (15 mph)	*– 1831*
All railroads designated post roads	*– 1838*
Rural Free Delivery Routes tested	*– 1896*
First experimental airmail flight	*– 1918*
Trial of submarine guided missile mail	*– 1959*
Same day Express Mail airport pickup service	*Now*

In spite of the sweeping changes in our transportation systems and our more recent leap from a mechanized world to automation, a surprising number of people still put a stamp on any kind of envelope, drop it in a box and expect it to get to its destination—a little like driving a rocket ship with a buggy whip.

Think about this: Even if you do follow the USPS addressing standards, your mail might be undeliverable. For example, the letter might go to the right company, but the intended receiver is no longer there. Did you know that once your letter is delivered to a business, the USPS has met its obligation? The business now acts as the agent for the addressee, and is *supposed* to forward your letter, if possible, or return it to you. Do you think every business has the staff to do this?

These are circumstances you can't control, but more often, your mail takes a detour because the delivery address is just plain wrong. These are circumstances you can control.

It's a fact.
More than 7% of all First-Class Mail is undeliverable.

2 *History of the United States Postal Service*, 1775-1993,
   U.S. Postal Service, September, 1993

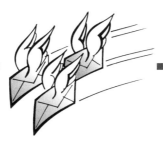

Smart Mail

Why does some mail get to its destination as swiftly as that famous Eagle flies, looking as good as the moment you sealed it? Why do you sometimes get a letter that looks as though it went through a threshing machine? And here's a real puzzler: Why do you sometimes get your own outgoing mail delivered back to you? Not returned, delivered.

If you still have such questions when you've finished this chapter, consider a visit to your nearest USPS Business Center. The experts there can unravel these and other mysteries for you, and help you design your mailing pieces and plan your mailing projects.

Superautomation

Within the next year or two, the USPS will completely reclassify the mail. Should you care? Absolutely. Today, Postal Service personnel look at your mail as part of the massive daily collection they face and ask three questions:

1. How much of this mail can be processed automatically?

2. How much of this mail can be processed mechanically?

3. How much do we have to do by hand?

Tomorrow those questions will be much simpler. A machine will check to see if your mail is *preferred, standard, automated or nonautomated*. It's a good guess preferred automated mail will get there first.

If you understand what the automated postal system needs from you, you're halfway into that elite, preferred company.

A Field Trip

Remember field trips? This one is for your mail.[3] (Many of the terms used on this trip are defined in the *Reference* and *Glossary.*) Here's the first letter you'll send:

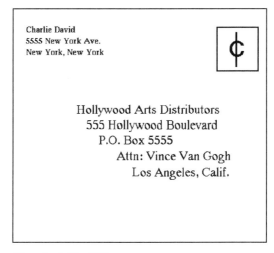

Charlie David
5555 New York Ave.
New York, New York

¢

Hollywood Arts Distributors
555 Hollywood Boulevard
P.O. Box 5555
Attn: Vince Van Gogh
Los Angeles, Calif.

Stamped, No ZIP

Pretty good. That's a typewritten address, an improvement over one that's hand-written. There's a return address and it has sufficient postage for First-Class Mail.

Let's see where it goes.

1. You drop it in a corner box. The mail carrier picks it up and puts it in a mail pouch.

2. At a collection point, your letter is put in a sack with mail from everybody else in your neighborhood.

3. At the incoming loading dock at your local P.O., the letter is routed to cancellation. The question comes up:

Is it metered?

---

3 Source: *mail flow planning system,* an interactive
software program, © 1994, U.S. Postal Service

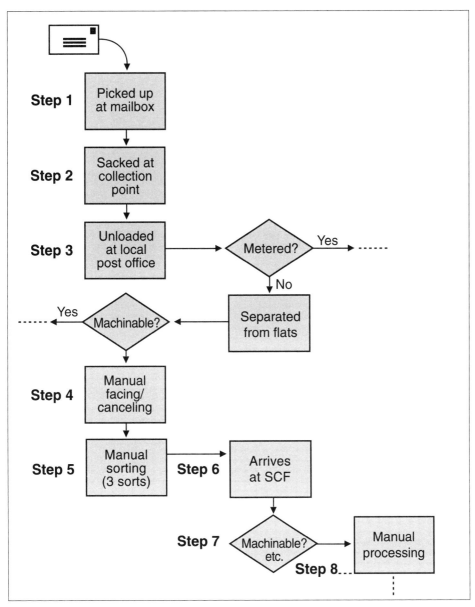

A Field Trip to the Post Office

It isn't, so it continues on its way to be culled—separated from the "flats" (big envelopes), packages or bundles. Now, the question is:

Is it machinable?

The answer is No, so it has to be *"faced"* and canceled by hand. *Facing* is a logical, if somewhat bizarre operation in which all the mail is turned to face the same way before it's canceled.

4. A postal worker turns the envelope and cancels the postage with a handheld mechanical device or a stamp.

5. The mail is sorted by hand by the first three digits and again by the last two.

For your letter, a postal worker has to stop turning and canceling mail to look up Vince's ZIP Code.

The two-level sort separates the local mail (the last two digits of the five-digit ZIP). Local mail is sorted again by a clerk to group the mail by carrier route. All the carrier has to do is sort it one more time into delivery sequence before getting started.

But Vince is in another city. The out-of-town mail is sent to the Sectional Center Facility (SCF) designated by the first three digits in the ZIP Code.

6. At the SCF inbound dock, your letter is unloaded with all the other letters the facility handles.

7. The receiving facility checks to see if it's:

Machinable?

OCR-Readable?

Metered?

Presorted?

Barcoded?

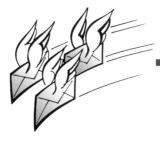

8. Being none of these things, your letter is shunted off to be sorted manually again, "the old-fashioned Ben Franklin way that's been around for 200 years," as a USPS Business Center expert puts it.

This whole process consumed the maximum time and peoplepower assigned to any letter mail. It's hard to believe it costs less than a cup of coffee.

> ***It's a fact.*** *The United States and Canada are tied for the least expensive First-Class Mail service in the world.*

Once More with...

This time through the postal system you'll give your letter a chance to keep up with some of the other mail.

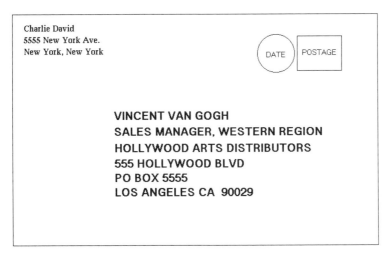

Charlie David
5555 New York Ave.
New York, New York

DATE   POSTAGE

**VINCENT VAN GOGH
SALES MANAGER, WESTERN REGION
HOLLYWOOD ARTS DISTRIBUTORS
555 HOLLYWOOD BLVD
PO BOX 5555
LOS ANGELES CA 90029**

*Machinable, OCR-Readable, Metered with a 5-digit ZIP
(not to scale)*

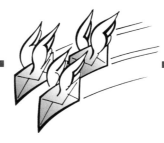

Machinable has to do with the size, thickness and weight of the letter. The USPS mechanized and automated equipment has certain tolerances for moving the mail along the chutes. (See "Mail Class, Sizes and Special Requirements" in this chapter.)

What makes this envelope machinable (a simplified answer)?

- It's a standard white #10 business envelope.

- It's about $^{15}/_{100}$ of an inch thick.

- It has postage on it.

- It's completely sealed.

> **Valentine's Day Massacre.** *Ask the good folks at your post office how they feel about the cute red envelope you send to your sweetheart.*

OCR-readable indicates the letter has the right attributes for an optical character reader to scan the front of the envelope.

How *could* this envelope be OCR-readable (another simplified answer)?

- You put the address where the machine expects it to be.

- The address is typed or machine printed in black ink with no overlapping or touching letters.

- The format is block left.

- You used sans serif type.

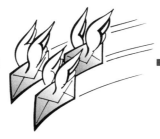

- The address is printed in upper case with no punctuation.

  The OCR can handle punctuation and some other fonts, but when it's flying at 10 letters a second, why slow it down?

- You used the correct abbreviation for boulevard and the official two-letter state code.

- There are no more than five lines in the readable address (the part from the company name down).

  You can have more lines, but they have to be above the address lines.

- The address lines are in the correct order, assuming you want this to go to the post office box.

Lines 1 and 2 are information lines. The address begins with line 3, the delivery name. The OCR-readable lines are Line 4 and 5, the delivery address lines, and Line 6, the city, state and ZIP.

The "Attn: Mr. Van Gogh" line has been moved to an information line where it won't interfere with the optical scanner. The OCR reads the envelope from the bottom up. If it sees a correct address, a built-in inkjet sprays the barcode equivalent of the ZIP Code+4 in the lower right corner of the envelope.

> **Attention: Mr. Jones.** *A possibly true story, much repeated in the Postal Service, tells of the unlucky post office in Jones, Maryland, that receives thousands of letters with Attention: Mr. (or Ms.) Jones as the last address line, where the City, State and ZIP go.*

To repeat, your letter *could* be OCR-readable, but USPS statistics show that only about half the envelopes with just the five-digit ZIP Codes are readable because of poor print quality or extraneous printing in the OCR read area.

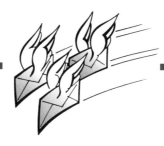

Because it is *metered* this envelope is put in a select group with other prepaid mail. Earlier, at the post office, you paid for a certain amount of postage; your meter was set to that amount. Permit mail and precanceled stamped envelopes work on the same principle. You make a deposit at the post office or buy precanceled stamps or envelopes. Prepaying gets you at least semi-automatic service:

1. This machinable, readable, metered and ZIP Coded letter stays with the first envelope up to Step 3, where the question is asked:

Is it metered?

4. The meter imprint and the standard size skip this letter three steps and into a separate group that bypasses the manual facing, canceling and sorting routine and starts a ride down the meter belt.

5. If your letter falls in the nonreadable half it goes to the Multi-Position Letter Sorting Machine (MPLSM).

   A postal worker operates this semi-automatic machine, keying in the information that triggers the three-digit sort. The operator can handle 50 to 60 letters a minute.

6. The letters go through the machine again at the same rate for the two-digit sort.

At the receiving post office, the letter takes similar giant steps to get ahead of the slower mail. The time-and-energy consumption factor for the whole tour is almost 50% less than the first time through.

Go back to Step 5. Say your letter makes it through the OCR station.

5. The OCR sprays the Delivery Point Barcode (DPBC) on your envelope and sends it to the barcode sorter (BCS).

6. The high-speed BCS, a fully automated system, does the primary and secondary sorts at 600 pieces a minute.

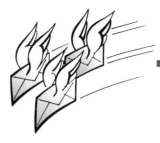

This route's efficiency is 93% better than mail that has to be handled manually.

Now you're getting someplace.

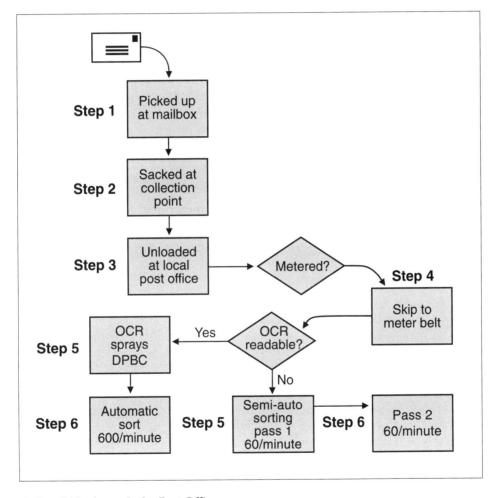

A Fast Ride through the Post Office

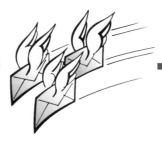

The World's Best Mail

If you're like many business people, you have such a strong instinct for competition, you'd hate to see your marketing mail languishing at the loading dock while your competitors' promo letters are zipping right by. Here's how to put your mail in the race at the head of the pack:

Machinable, Readable, Prebarcoded, Presorted, Metered and Trayed with ZIP+4

Database software sorts your letters by ZIP Code and within the ZIP Code, by company name so you can check for duplicates before you meter this batch.

When the post office gets this envelope, it whips through the system 97.97% more efficiently than the first envelope.[4]

The big bonus is if you mail a lot of these at one time, you're eligible for excellent discounts. (See "List Management Software" in the *Reference* to learn about tools for even greater efficiency and discounts.)

---

4 Efficiency factors based on USPS estimates of labor and time.

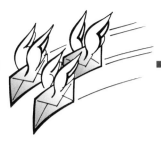

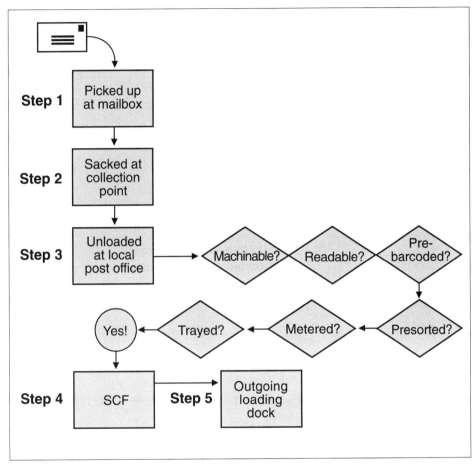

The USPS Bullet Train

Big Iron

Take a closer look at the heavy machinery that replaces some of the tedious manual handling your first letter went through. Because you prepared your mail right, your mail got to use this great equipment.

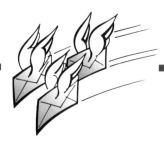

Advanced Facer-Canceler: This machine properly positions each piece so all addresses and stamps face in the same direction, then cancels the postage and separates the mail for further processing. The facer-canceler also reads Facing Identification Mark (FIM) patterns on business reply and courtesy reply mail. For more on FIMs, see *Business Reply Mail* later in this chapter.

> ***Let 'er Rip!*** *According to an inside source at the USPS, these machines go so fast, there is a designated area nearby called the rip-up section for the tubs of ripped up mail that accumulates every night. The USPS makes every effort to put damaged pieces back together and deliver them, as you may have noticed when you received one of these casualties in the mail. The rip-up section's regular visitors are letters with loose flaps, lumpy promotional gimmicks and self-mailers that come untabbed.*

Barcode Sorter (BCS): The BCS reads the barcodes and sorts the mail at the fast clip of 10 per second. When you prebarcode your mail it bypasses the OCR and goes directly to this machine. This saves the USPS time and money, and who knows? It could help keep the rates down.

> ***Fade Out.*** *If you prebarcode your mail with your PC and laser printer, be sure the toner cartridge in your printer is fresh. Print density is critical to the OCR's success.*

Because you put the ZIP+4 on the envelope, this machine can sort your mail right down to the carrier's route. The next improvements to the system will allow automatic sorting by machine right to the carrier's bin in *walk sequence* (the order of delivery).

> ***Pizzazz for your ZIPs.*** *For your PC-driven mailing list, the USPS offers a one-time free ZIP+4 Coding. The USPS will also verify your 5-digit ZIP Codes, street and city names.*

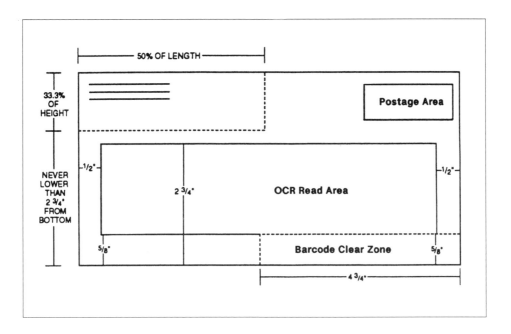

The OCR Read/Barcode Clear Zone—Courtesy of the U.S. Postal Service

Optical Character Reader: To recap, the OCR reads machine-printed addresses on letter mail, gives it a Delivery Point Barcode on the lower right corner, and does an initial sort based on the barcode just printed—all at the rate of 10 pieces per second.

To read the delivery address, the OCR has to find it, and it won't if you don't put the entire address within the *OCR read area.* You also have to keep

extraneous print out of the read area. For example, if the machine sees your return address in this area and the delivery address is not dark enough, your own letter could be delivered right back to you.

Make sure there's good contrast between the ink and the background on the envelope or label, and that the letters are far enough apart for the OCR to distinguish between them. For better scanning, avoid printing on "pulpy" paper that has dark fibers in it that might be mistaken for print, or paper so thin that the printing inside shows through the envelope.

> **Inside Tip.** *Postal Service barcodes always appear in the lower right corner. Barcodes preprinted by the sender can be displayed in that same corner or immediately above or below the address block.*

Remote Barcode Sorter (RBCS): At the Sectional Center Facility, mail that can't be read by the OCR is coded on the back and held in a staging area. The RBCS sends an image of the face of the mailpiece to a computer screen for editing. An operator adds missing information or corrects errors. The image is returned to the OCR for reprocessing and barcoding.

Wide Area Barcode Reader: This machine reads barcodes anywhere in the wider *barcode read area* that gives more flexibility in where the barcode can be positioned, but also restricts the area you can use for teasers on a standard envelope. One way to fool the system is to print your teasers on an angle and in italic type, or in a light color, or put them above or below the read area.

Big Mail

You learned a fair amount about address formats on the field trip to the post office. Because it is so critical to the smooth running of your mailing operation, especially now that you're going to be mailing hundreds of letters at a time, take a closer look at addressing and some of the more important rules about the appearance of your mail.

Main Information Blocks and Their Placements

A mailing envelope of any size consists of five information blocks that fit into specific areas.

■ The *return address* goes in the upper left corner of the envelope. It can be no more than one-third the height of the mailpiece and no more than one-half the width.

If you send your letter third-class with no return address and it's not deliverable, the Postal Service throws it away immediately.

If your First-Class letter can't be delivered and there's no return address on the envelope, it goes to the Dead Letter office. It may wait there for months before the Postal Service can open it to look for an inside address. (They really do this sometimes.)

Print *special messages* or instructions (for example, "Time-Dated Material—Open Immediately") below the return address. Leave a clear space—at least ¼ inch—between the two.

■ Put *postage*—stamps, meter imprint or permit imprint—in the upper right corner.

The rules for the permit imprint are very specific. You have to establish an advance deposit account with the USPS before you can use one. The imprint language is dictated by the permit type and cannot vary. You can get a wide variety of permits, including First-Class Mail, presorted First-Class Mail, priority mail, mailgram, third-class and fourth-class bulk rate.

The permit imprint can be produced by a printing press, lithograph, mimeograph, hand stamp, but it can't be typewritten or hand drawn. Your PC printer qualifies as a printing press provided the quality is very good.

- Remember to position the *mailing address* so it falls completely within the OCR read area.

Make sure the address is complete and accurate. At least the addressee's company name, delivery address line, city, state and ZIP Code are required, with each word spelled correctly. ZIP+4 is required for a discount.

If a street address contains a geographic directional, such as East or Northwest, make sure it's included. "MAIN ST" won't do if the full address is E MAIN ST or MAIN ST NW.

Follow the USPS standard format for addresses:

- Make all lines flush left in the address block.

- Unless you prebarcode your mail, machine-print all letters in capitals without punctuation (except for the hyphen in the ZIP+4 Code), special characters or multiple blanks.

- The OCR "prefers" two spaces after the address before the ZIP Code. The OCR also needs what the USPS calls a "simple sans serif typeface."

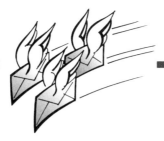

- If there isn't enough space on the delivery address line for a room, suite, box or apartment number, put that information on a new line *above* the delivery address.

- Instead of creating a new line, you can condense some of the information, using standard USPS abbreviations.

- *Abbreviations:* The USPS has official abbreviations for street designators and even some business titles and other words. The right abbreviation gives your mail the best chance for OCR-readability.

  Always use the standard postal abbreviation for states (CT, not Conn. or Ct.; PA, not Penna. or Pa.). Freelance abbreviating will only delay your mail.

  When the OCR reads the address, it searches its files for a match. If it doesn't find one, your letter is rejected.

- Keep the *Barcode Clear Zone* at the lower right part of the envelope free of printing of any kind. If you prebarcode your mail, you can use this area or place the code above or below the address block.

- *Presort:* If you have the volume needed for presorting, you can get a discount. Your mail also has to be bundled and labeled. See your local post office for specifics.

  > ***z-z-z-Z-I-P!*** *Make a habit of using the full ZIP+4 on your mail; your letters zip right through the system and earn a discount.*

- *Prebarcoding:* In addition to discounts, prebarcoding has other advantages. First, the address text of barcoded mail doesn't have to be

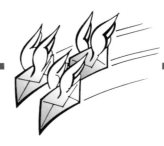

OCR-readable. The machine looks for a barcode first and if it finds one, it processes the piece and moves on. That gives you more latitude in the aesthetics of your mailpieces, including the use of upper and lower case letters, logos, flowing script and brightly colored inks.

Addressing

Let's put these addressing principles to work. One record in your list reads:

Ms. April Showers
Purchasing Director
Acme Amalgamated International, Inc.
28652 South Hammondville Boulevard
Industrial Park
Wherever, NY 12345-8976

There are problems with this address.

- There are six lines in the address. Most label templates do well with five-line addresses, but run into trouble with more. You could put the title after the name.

- The company name is pretty long for a label, as well. You'll have to abbreviate it.

- The line above the City, State, ZIP *must* be the delivery point address; that is, the address that directs the postal worker who delivers it. Who gets the mail at Industrial Park?

It might seem more efficient to shorten the customer's title to PUR DIR, part of the company name to INTL, and a part of the street name to PK.

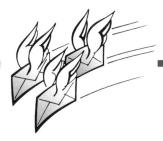

However, the abbreviations used here, although perhaps not all familiar, conform with Postal Service addressing standards.[5]

MS APRIL SHOWERS PURCHNG DIR

ACME AMALGAMATED INTRNTL INC

INDUSTRIAL PARK

28652 S HAMMONDVILLE BLVD

WHEREVER NY 12345-8976

A better address would include the specific mailstop location—Building 19, Suite 607—in the address. This information obviously won't fit on the delivery address line, so you add it to the line just above the delivery address. Now your piece reads:

MS APRIL SHOWERS PURCHNG DIR

ACME AMALGAMATED INTRNTL INC

INDUSTRIAL PARK BLDG 19 STE 607

28652 S HAMMONDVILLE BLVD

WHEREVER NY 12345-8976

All lines are flush left, all letters are capitals, there are no multiple blanks and the only punctuation is the hyphen in the ZIP+4 Code. The address is complete and correct.

The addressing standards just covered apply to all mail, but what else do you need to know for your entire kit to be Postally Correct?

---

5 *Postal Addressing Standards,* Publication 28, USPS, January 1992

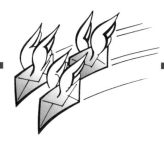

Mail Classes, Sizes and Special Requirements

As you know, the USPS classifies every piece of mail as express, priority, First-Class, second-class, third-class, fourth-class, parcel post and so on. The USPS *Domestic Mail Manual* tells absolutely everything you need to know about each kind in great detail. For more concise reading on the subject, check "Recommended Reading" in the *Reference* for the names of some excellent guides and aids published by the U.S. Postal Service.

For your purposes, concentrate on the letters and marketing pieces you've designed to grow your business. You can start with these general rules:

■ Regardless of class, all addressed mail pieces must be at least .007 inch thick. If the piece is less than ¼ inch thick, it has to be rectangular and at least 3½ by 5 inches.

■ Single piece correspondence up to 11 ounces qualifies for the current First-Class postal *rate* (the price of a stamp). First-Class Mail *service* applies to any eligible mail up to 70 pounds.

■ Second-class mail requires advance USPS approval and is available for only certain types of publications, such as a nonprofit newsletter. (See "Newsletters" in this chapter.)

■ Mail weighing up to 16 ounces is eligible for third-class postal rates. First-Class and third-class rates are the same up to 11 ounces (at this writing) so third-class saves nothing on single pieces unless they exceed that weight.

■ Third-class *bulk* rates for identical pieces from one to 16 ounces can save a lot of money.

■ Oversize envelopes (flats) up to 11 ounces are eligible for First-Class rates and for third-class rates up to 16 ounces.

- To get special bulk rates, weight, quantity, dimensions and thickness requirements must be met for each category.

  The maximum weight for ZIP+4 Coded letters or postcards is 2.5 ounces. Prebarcoded letters or cards can weigh up to 3 ounces.

  You'll need several hundred pieces of the same type and size to qualify for bulk rates. The actual number of pieces required and other specifications vary according to the class of service you specify. Check with your local post office for current requirements.

- The best *rate* for any class is given to mail presorted down to the carrier route code.

- The best *service* is given to mail that can be automated.

Be sure to check with your post office before you finalize your mailing plans. Here are some recommendations for mailing your desktop marketing kit components:

Letters and Cards

Use First-Class Mail for letters and postcards weighing 11 ounces or less. The dimensions of a *letter* must be 3½ to 6⅛ inches vertically and 5 to 11½ inches horizontally.

If you design your *postcard* right, it costs less than a letter. The postcard must be no smaller than 3½ by 5 inches and no larger than 4¼ by 6 inches to qualify for the lower rate. If the card is larger than that, it has to carry the full First-Class rate and you can't use the word Postcard on it. As the card gets larger, there are further requirements for thickness. Check with your post office before you print.

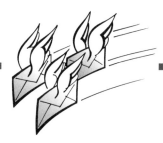

Large Mailing Envelopes

Large mailing envelopes (flats) include envelopes larger than standard business envelopes, magazines, catalogs and other similar pieces. If you want this mail to go First-Class, print First-Class on the outside. (You could use a green-diamond bordered envelope, but it might clash with your design.)

Machine-Friendly Flats: You can get the same range of discounts and services for your large envelopes as for letter mail. For a machinable piece, your flats must be no smaller than 6 by 6 inches and no larger than 12 by 15 inches, with thickness from .009 to .075 inches.

Don't send:

- mailpieces that are too stiff or too flexible (as defined by the USPS). They'll surely land in the rip-up tubs.

- envelopes containing protruding promotion gimmicks, such as keys or pens.

- polywrapped or shrink-wrapped pieces (without consulting the local post office staff).

Self-Mailers

Newsletters, circulars and similar mailpieces, when folded, sealed and mailed without an envelope are called self-mailers. Your tri-fold mailer fits in this category and in the next one too, if it has a perforated bounceback device.

- For a single-sheet self-mailer sealed with one tab, use a minimum weight of 28-pound stock.

- For a single or multiple sheet mailer sealed with two tabs, you can cut the stock weight to as low as 20 pounds.

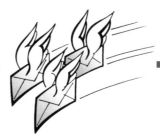

- Instead of tabs, you can use wafer seals, tape or glue if you prefer. (Wafer seals are round seals affixed flat, not folded over like a tab. They can be decorative, emblem-like sealers.)

> **Staples.** *Be kind to your USPS helpers and don't use staples—they hurt! They also jam the machines. You should also know that you can't get an automation discount for mail with staples.*

Reply Devices

Business Reply Mail (BRM) is a postage-paid envelope or card customers use to respond to your mailing.

- The self-mailer as BRM has to include instructions for sealing it.

- For a small mailing, you can meter the reply mail. Turn off the date so the response can come back any time.

- For a larger mailing, save money with a Business Reply Mail permit.

  You can get a permit by opening a deposit account at the post office and paying a fee for the permit. You pay only for pieces that are actually returned to you, plus a small service fee. In contrast, once you've metered or stamped a business reply piece, you've used the postage even if you don't get a response.

Courtesy Reply Mail (CRM) is like Business Reply Mail without the prepaid postage. A Courtesy Reply envelope simplifies and speeds up bill paying for your customers and hastens their return through the postal system. Unlike a BRM, you don't need a permit for Courtesy Reply Mail.

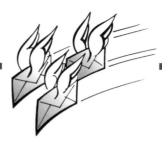

All reply mail must follow strict guidelines for layout and imprinting. There is no leeway for the language or placement of the elements of a BRM or CRM. You need a Facing Identification Mark (FIM) and preprinted barcode, which you can get without charge from your local post office, if your equipment can't produce them.

> **Crunch.** *The Postal Service recommends folding double-postcards and self-mailers at the bottom edge so they are machinable and won't come apart during processing. They stand a much better chance of making it past the rip-up section.*
>
> *If you seal the piece at the top, change the orientation of the inside pages to make them easy to follow.*

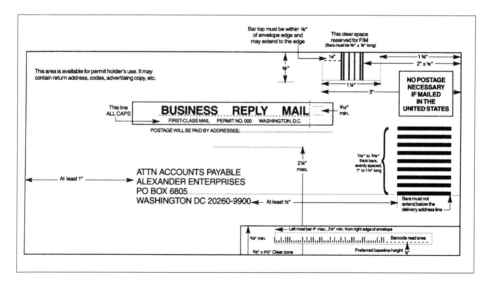

The Elements of Reply Mail—Courtesy of the U.S. Postal Service

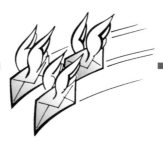

Newsletters

If you plan to publish regularly or can meet the requirements for recognition as a nonprofit organization, you can apply to receive the special discounts for periodicals. Ask your local postmaster about other privileges extended to publishers and nonprofit organizations.

Newspapers, magazines and other periodicals sold by subscription can qualify for second-class mailing privileges. This class is restricted to publishers the Postal Service has approved, so find out early before you plan to mail.

If your business is not approved for second-class mail, use First-Class or third-class mail for your newsletter. For really heavy reading, use fourth-class mail (which includes parcel post and printed matter weighing more than one pound).

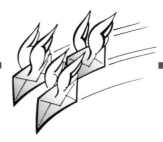

Checklist for Bulk Mailing

✔ Apply for the permit from your post office.

✔ Find out from the post office the current minimum quantity for bulk mail and ask for the mailing regulations and instruction publications.

✔ Get your official camera-ready art for the barcodes for reply mail from your local post office unless you can produce it with your equipment.

✔ Prepare the outer envelope or label and the reply devices first.

✔ Show Business Reply Mail pieces and other preprinted mail-formatted pieces to the postmaster for approval. They must meet regulations for identification marks and clear areas. Pick up your USPS mailing trays.

✔ Sort and print your mail; make sure every piece faces the same way.

✔ Band the mail by ZIP groups and place it in trays.

✔ Fill out a Statement of Mailing form.

✔ Return the trays and form to the post office that issued your permit.

So now your mail is speeding on its way. We look forward to hearing from you.

Reference

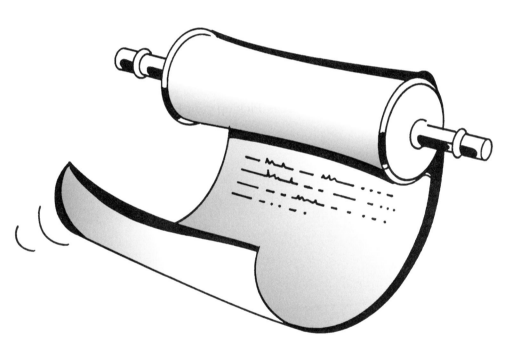

Reference

This section is a collection of information about the design, production and delivery of PC-generated business mail. Here you'll find:

- A [Very] Short Course on Personal Computing

- A guide to Desktop Mailing Tools

- Resources for mail-related products and services

- Postally Correct Miscellany

- The *Mail It!* Library

- A Glossary of design, marketing, production and delivery terms

A [Very] Short Course In Personal Computing

If your publications still look like they come out of a standard typewriter, here's a short course on why you should stop using your computer like your old Remington. (If you're still using the Remington, face facts and switch to a PC.) If you already know the basics, you don't need this section.

Any PC can do the things discussed in this book. All your Mac, Windows or DOS PC needs is the right software. A good array of startup programs should include a word processor for writing (AmiPro, MacWrite Pro, Microsoft Word, WordPerfect…), and might include a spreadsheet program for numbers (Lotus 1-2-3, Microsoft Excel, QuattroPro…), a database program for lists (FileMaker Pro, Microsoft Access, FoxPro…) and a graphics package for presentations and extra clip art (Aldus Persuasion, Microsoft PowerPoint…) or original art (Adobe Illustrator, Aldus Freehand, Corel Draw!…).

At this writing, most word processors still offer limited capabilities for overlaying text on graphics or the reverse, so for complex multilayered integration of words and pictures, add a page composition program like Aldus PageMaker, QuarkXpress or Ventura Publisher go to your software library. Microsoft Publisher is a simpler low-cost page composition program that's especially good for beginners.

Using any one of these software programs, you can:

- record (save) whatever you type

- recall recorded information

- change and rearrange the material

- re-record it, either as an original or a copy

- send it to a printer for hard copy (the printed page)

Getting Started

A computer user of considerable experience and skill said recently, *"Nothing frustrates me more than buying a new software package and then getting stuck trying to figure out how to get a new project started. I know how to install the software, but just try to find the next step in the manual!"*

You won't learn how to run your computer here, but you'll get a high-level look at how certain operations work. If this short course doesn't help, try a classroom introductory course on PCs.

Here are the three things you have to know to get started:

- how to start the computer

- how to start the software application program

- how to start a new project (document file)

Here are the five next most important things you have to know to use any new software:

- how to quit

- how to get out of trouble

- how to navigate

- how to save your work

- how to find your work once it's saved

Once you know that much, this is what you have to know to work on a specific project:

- Is this a new project?

- Is this a revision of an old one?

- What's it called?

- Where do we keep it?

The basic concepts that make these questions clear are often omitted or hard to find in software user guides. Let's fill in some of the blanks.

Disk Drives and Operating Systems

Your computer has at least two drives, a floppy and a hard drive. Today the floppy drive might actually be a slot for a tiny credit card-shaped PC card, but in any case it's a drive for removable storage media.

When you turn on the computer, the built-in *operating system* (such as DOS, Windows or System 7) that lives on the hard disk inside the box gives instructions to the parts of the computer to get ready to be used. Once the system is up and running, you can start a *software application program,* such as Microsoft Word or Lotus 1-2-3, which is most likely installed on your hard disk.

When you give the program's startup command, the parts you need are loaded from the hard drive into the computer's volatile memory, sometimes called Random Access Memory (RAM). Once your application program is running, you can open a file that's stored on disk or start a new one.

Directories and Folders

Once you save your work, how are you going to get it back? You *have* to know where it's stored. In some programs, the software installation process creates a directory for your work and tells you where it is. But others leave it up to you, so you have to learn something about directories or folders.

On any computer, a directory or subdirectory is just a place to keep files. Macintosh computers call the directories folders; subdirectories are folders-within-folders. Computer manufacturers are fond of the metaphor of directory-as-filing-cabinet, but the computer directory/folder is much more useful. On your computer, you can see all the names of your files at once and retrieve them by name.

To see a directory or folder listing of files:

- On a DOS system, at the system prompt (C:>), type DIR and ENTER.

- On a Windows system double-click the mouse on the File Cabinet icon (picture) in the Main window of Program Manager. Program Manager is usually the first thing you see when you start Windows.

- On a Mac, double-click the mouse on the hard disk icon on the desktop (the screen). Then double-click any folder icon you see.

What the Filenames Mean

The names of the files in your directories and folders are important to you. Virtually any software program has two kinds of files: data files and program files. The program files are the ones that perform all the functions advertised— the ones you install more-or-less permanently on your hard drive. Data files are the text, spreadsheets and presentations you make yourself after starting the

program and typing the words, entering the numbers or drawing the pictures. You can save your data files on the hard drive or on floppy disks.

DOS Program Filenames	*DOS Data Filenames*
word.exe	letter.doc
excel.exe	march.xls
ppt.exe	rally.ppt

On the Windows and Mac systems, look for little symbols to tell you the filetype. Both use a miniature page for data files. Windows uses an icon shaped like a little screen for program files. Mac's symbol is a diamond-shaped icon. Windows also uses DOS filenames.

Program files stay in the background and don't change as you use them. It's pretty hard to damage them. Even if you do, you can just reinstall the software and start over. Data files are a different story. They're easily changed, easily damaged and oh, so easily lost. It's important to learn how to change them without damaging them and how to store them without losing them.

You may spend $400 on your new software program. How much do you think you spend in time and effort making those data files or looking for them?

The Startup Command

Starting an application is easy but it can look a little different on different computers. Your computer may be set up for you to display a special menu so all you have to do is choose an option from a list. (Point to it with the mouse or arrow key and press ENTER.)

On a graphical user interface system (GUI) like Windows or the Mac, you can just double-click the mouse on the icon representing the program. For

example, in Windows, double-click the flying W to start Microsoft Word. You can also double-click on a filename in a directory or folder to load both the file and the program.

For DOS systems, certain application programs put a special batch file (such as WP.BAT) on the hard disk during the installation process. All you have to do is type the first part of the filename, WP, and ENTER and the program is loaded automatically. Look for .BAT files in your directories.

RAM

When the computer is on and the application program is in memory (RAM), the work you do, like typing a letter, will also sort of float around in RAM until you save it. Before you save and close the file you're working on, you can change it, rearrange it or quit and start over.

Unfortunately, while it's in memory you can also accidentally scramble it, delete it or trash it in ways that haven't even been invented yet. As soon as you save it (store it on a disk) it's relatively safe. You can save your work either to the hard drive or to a floppy or both. As long as you give it a name no other file shares, it's safe.

Getting Out of Trouble

The first thing to do with any new package after you get it started is to figure out how to shut it down. Check out the screen to find Save, Close and Quit or Exit (usually on the File menu). Try starting and stopping a few times so you're comfortable with the routine. It goes a long way toward giving you confidence.

Next, explore the menu system, screen and keyboard to find Escape, Cancel and Undo. ESC is usually a key, Cancel is often a choice in a pop-up box and Undo is most often on the Edit menu. Now find Help, usually the F1 key or an icon or menu or all three. Now you're ready for some real work.

If your system freezes or crashes, you'll have to restart it and lose anything you've typed since you last saved. Before you turn off the system, remove any floppy disks unless the light is still on on that drive.

Try It:

1. *Turn on your computer.*
2. *Look at a directory.*
3. *Start an application.*
4. *Find Help.*
5. *Close and quit the application.*
6. *Turn off the computer.*

When you know how to find Help and get out of the program, you're ready to…

Start a New Project:

1. Start your word processing application.
   Open a *new* file.

2. Type something.

3. Save the file.

   Some programs ask you to name the file before you open it, some after and some not until you close it. It's a good idea to name it at the earliest opportunity.

Naming is part of the save routine. The first time, you'll get a chance to say where you want to save it. After that, it's automatically saved to the same folder or directory unless you specify something else.

4. Close it.

5. Quit.

Now open a file you made earlier:

1. Start your WP program again.

2. Give the command to open an existing file, not a new one.

3. Specify the directory it's in.

4. Specify the name you gave it.

Some programs do the steps in a different order, but each step is required.

There are several ways to "specify": Type the name and ENTER or click OK; point to the name on a list (highlight it) and click the mouse or press ENTER.

When the file is on your screen, you can review it, print it or make changes. Here's the great part.

If you want to "grandfather" your files—that is, keep several older backup versions for revision history and disaster recovery:

1. Choose Save as…to save the file.

2. Give the file a new name and ENTER or click OK.

On the other hand, to update your master copy of the file…

1. Choose Save.

2. Keep the same name.

3. ENTER or OK.

The system stores the file over the original, which is gone forever.

Computing Tips.

- *If you choose an option or give a command and nothing happens, press ENTER or mouse-click the OK button so the computer knows it's supposed to do something.*

- *Save and close your files before you exit a program.*

- *Quit all programs before you turn off the computer.*

- *Wait until the system stops "working" before you turn it off.*

- *Never risk more than fifteen minutes work. Save!*

If you understand this much about computers, you can learn the rest as you practice. It takes a lot of practice to become proficient.

Desktop Mailing Tools

Computers have gotten smarter and so has the USPS automated equipment. It stands to reason that software developers would find ways to bring the two together.

List Management Software

Now that more companies are generating barcoded database-driven mailings from the desktop, many new programs have been developed to make sure those barcodes and addresses are accurate, up to date and appropriate for your marketing program. Here are a few:

AddressMate

AddressMate is compatible with the most popular word processing and database programs. It works in two modes: Design and Database. You can use the program as a stand-alone or attach it to your WP program.

□	**F**ile	**E**dit	**V**iew	**I**nsert	F**o**rmat	**T**ools	Ta**b**le	**W**indow	**H**elp	A**m**ate

AddressMate icon on a word processing menu bar
—Courtesy of Co-Star Corporation

One of this program's most useful features is address capture. You can save those shell letter inside addresses to the built-in AddressMate database and let the program's Intelligent Address Recognition sort out which bits of data to put into which database fields.

AddressMate's database can be customized in minor ways, but works well with other database programs if you need more flexibility.

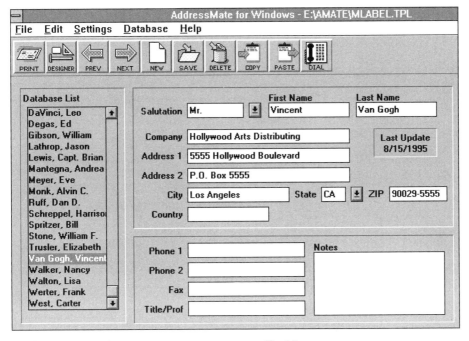

Address capture is a great way to save one-off addresses.

SmartMailer Addressing Software

Pitney Bowes' SmartMailer Addressing Software is a full-featured program used to compile and produce a database-formatted mail list, presort it, detect and eliminate duplicate records, and configure and print presorted envelopes, labels and cards. It's most important feature is validating the ZIP Codes in your existing databases and correcting them, if necessary.

If you use rented mailing lists, the reporting function will be especially useful in showing the number of duplicates and bad addresses.

Here's a quick look at some of the features of SmartMailer Addressing Software:

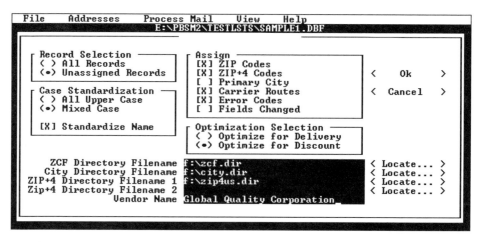

Postal Coding for SmartMailer—Courtesy of Pitney Bowes, Inc.

Postal Coding: With the companion compact data disc (CD-ROM) *ZIP+4 and Carrier Route Address Directory,* you can use the Postal Coding module to code your list with USPS CASS-certified ZIP Codes. (See CASS in the *Glossary.*) The system will try to code with the Delivery Point Barcode plus the Carrier Route code. If it is unable to complete the coding, an error message gives you the reason so you can correct the address. SmartMailer tries to help by offering suggestions. The CD-ROM directory is updated every three months with official USPS codes.

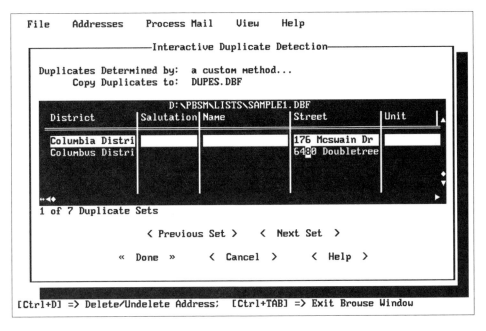

Dupe Detect for SmartMailer

Duplicate Detection: Databases eventually acquire duplicate records, most of which are either the same name with different addresses or different spellings of the same name at one address. You might inadvertently update different versions of the same record. Dupe Detect identifies those versions and offers you the chance to save data from the copies into the main record before you get rid of the duplicates.

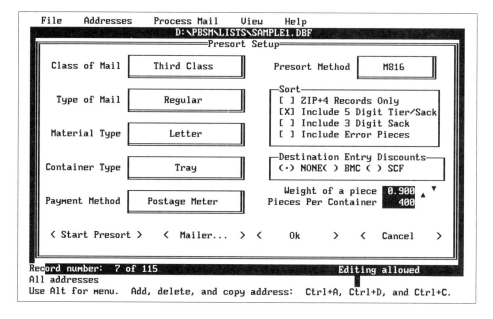

```
 File     Addresses    Process Mail    View     Help
                   D:\PBSM\LISTS\SAMPLE1.DBF
╔══════════════════════Presort Setup══════════════════════╗

   Class of Mail    │ Third Class │    Presort Method  │  M816  │

                                     ┌─Sort─────────────────────┐
   Type of Mail     │   Regular   │   │ [ ] ZIP+4 Records Only   │
                                     │ [X] Include 5 Digit Tier/Sack│
                                     │ [ ] Include 3 Digit Sack │
   Material Type    │   Letter    │   │ [ ] Include Error Pieces │
                                     └──────────────────────────┘
                                     ┌─Destination Entry Discounts─┐
   Container Type   │    Tray     │   │ (·) NONE( ) BMC ( ) SCF  │
                                     └──────────────────────────┘
                                        Weight of a piece  │0.900│ ▲ ▼
   Payment Method   │Postage Meter│     Pieces Per Container│  400│

   < Start Presort >    <  Mailer... >  <      Ok       >   <    Cancel    >

 Record number:   7 of 115                          Editing allowed
 All addresses
 Use Alt for menu.   Add, delete, and copy address:   Ctrl+A, Ctrl+D, and Ctrl+C.
```

Presort for SmartMailer

Presort: In the Presort program, you choose the class of mail you want and the type of mailing piece you're sending. You can specify tray packing or another type of container, and indicate your method of payment.

SmartMailer Reports: The SmartMailer reports are useful for managing your mailing program as well as for compiling information for the paperwork required by the Postal Service. This program can even print labels for your bulk mail containers.

```
                    Facsimile Postage Report
                    Smart Mailer Presort 3.30.3
                    ─────────────────────────────

                         d:\dbf2\fcm1
                    08-07-1995      10:30:39


                                Count      Net Rate        Postage
First Class (None)              Pieces    (per piece)      Charges
─────────────                   ──────    ───────────   ─────────────
5-Digit Barcoded Rate            1000      0.258        $       258.00
3-Digit Barcoded Rate             720      0.264        $       190.08
Presort First Class Rate           80      0.274        $        21.92
Nonpresorted Barcoded Rate        200      0.305        $        61.00
Single Piece Rate                   1      0.320        $         0.32
                                                        ─────────────
Subtotal Postage Due                                    $       531.32
                                                        ─────────────
TOTAL POSTAGE DUE FOR MAILING                           $       531.32


Postal Savings
──────────────
Cost of Mailing without Presort                         $       640.32
Cost of Mailing with Presort                            $       531.32
                                                        ─────────────
Postage Savings Due to Presort                          $       109.00
```

SmartMailer Presort Summary Report

Market Analysis Software

Your home-grown or rented database can be made even more valuable by subjecting it to sophisticated computerized market analysis.

Geographic Information Systems (GIS) can give you statistics about your list, segmented by industry, buying habits, education and more. Locations can be pinpointed down to the block level. Representative GIS software:

Conquest for Windows
Atlas GIS for Windows
Strategic Mapping, Inc.
3135 Kifer Road
Santa Clara, CA 95051
408-970-9600

MapInfo
Streetinfo
MapInfo Corporation
One Global View
Troy, NY 12180
1-800-327-8627

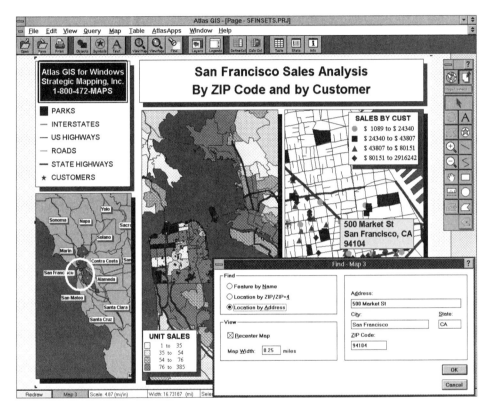

Market analysis software adds value to your list.

Atlas GIS for Windows—Courtesy of Strategic Mapping, Inc.

Specialized Printers for Mailing

Printing mailing envelopes and labels in quantity can tie up your office printer for too long. Some companies solve this problem by adding a specialty printer dedicated to their database-driven marketing.

Direct Address Envelope Printers

Most desktop laser and inkjet printers can print addresses and even barcodes directly on envelopes at speeds ranging from about 6 to 10 pages per minute. Envelopes take longer, but the speed still may be adequate for very small mailings.

If you plan regular mass mailings, though, you might consider a specialty desktop printer just for your mailing operation. Some of these printers can print barcoded addresses on envelopes or postcards in sizes ranging from 3½ inches up to 12 x 24 flats. Speeds are impressive: more than 83 envelopes and close to 60 flats—9 x 12 envelopes—a minute. Representative direct address envelope printers:

W700 Addressing System
W890 Addressing System
Pitney Bowes, Inc.
One Elmcroft Road
Stamford, CT 06926-0700
1-800-MR BOWES X4757

RENA Systems, Inc.
290 Hansen Access Road
King of Prussia, PA 19406-2467
1-800-426-7904

Label Printers

Your laser or inkjet printer can also do sheets of labels at a speed of 6 to 10 pages a minute. Aligned three-up, that's a lot of labels, but it's not so convenient for one-offs.

A specialty label printer can free your main office printer for day-to-day work. These printers can print a variety of label sizes at speeds ranging from 60 one-inch labels a minute to more than 80 four-up labels a minute. The smallest of the printers is only $4\frac{1}{2}$ by $6\frac{1}{4}$ by 7 inches. Representative specialty label printers:

LabelWriter XL
LabelWriter XL Plus
Co-Star Corporation
100 Field Point Road
Greenwich, CT 06830-6406

TCP 615
TCP 625
Taneum Computer Products, Inc.
203 Southwest 41st Street
Renton, WA 97055
206-251-0711

Postage Meters

Postage meters are used to pay for postage in advance and print the amount directly on the mailing piece when it is used. Many postage meters today can print in increments of one-tenth of a cent, which can add up to big savings for bulk mailing.

If you don't have a postage meter for your business, here are some good reasons to get one:

- A meter gives your mail a professional image.

- You can order a special slug for your meter to imprint a message or slogan as you meter each mailing piece.

- Meters save money. You don't waste postage because you can always use just the correct amount.

- The Postal Service waives the bulk application fee if you use your own meter.

> **OOPS.** *If you forget to reset the postage from a letter you sent priority mail, for example, are you out of luck? No. Just save the envelope and take it to your post office, where you can get a partial refund (up to 90 percent).*
>
> *In contrast, if you knocked over a cup of coffee onto a sheet of stamps, you would be out of luck—no stamps, no refund, no coffee.*

To use a postage meter you need a license, which you can get from your local post office. Every meter has to be inspected periodically; take your machine to the post office to be examined (a USPS requirement). The meter is checked to make sure it's operating correctly and hasn't been tampered with.

To ensure the integrity of the U.S. Postal Service revenue, meters are rented (leased), not sold. Only four manufacturers are licensed by the USPS to manufacture and lease postage meters:

- Ascom Hasler Mailing Systems Inc.
  19 Forest Parkway
  Shelton, CT 06484-0903

- Friden Neopost
  30955 Huntwood
  Hayward, CA 94544-7005

- Pitney Bowes, Inc.
  1 Elmcroft Road
  Stamford, CT 06926-0700

- Postalia Inc.
  1980 University Lane
  Lisle, IL 60532-2152

Pitney Bowes is the largest manufacturer authorized to lease meters to the public.

Remote Meter-Setting Systems

A relatively new service for adding postage to your meter without leaving your office is especially welcome to the small business and home office entrepreneur. You never have to run out of postage again. Here's how it works:

- You set up a deposit account in a designated bank.

- The meter company assigns a password to you.

- When you're about to need postage, call the meter-setting service.

- Enter the password, your meter number and the amount of postage you need.

- Your meter is reset.

Representative meter-setting system:

Postage-By-Phone
Pitney Bowes, Inc.
One Elmcroft Road
Stamford, CT 06926-0700
1-800-MR BOWES X4757

Resources

The explosion of desktop marketing activities has encouraged many companies to bring exciting new products and services to market. These resources are listed here.

Associations

Direct Marketing Association, Inc. (DMA)
1120 Avenue of the Americas
New York, NY 10036-6700
Phone: 212 768-7277
FAX: 212 768-4546

DMA keeps members informed about new printing technology, media techniques, and postal regulations through seminars, conferences and monthly publications such as *Washington Update, Washington Alert* and *Direct Line.*

Through the DMA Library and Resource Center you have access to resources for finding reliable answers to complex questions. DMA publishes a list of books relating to direct marketing, with special pricing for members.

Newsletter Publishers Association (NPA)
1401 Wilson Boulevard
Suite 207
Arlington, VA 22209
Phone: 703 527-2333, 1-800-356-9302
FAX: 703 841-0629

The NPA's goal is to further the professional, economic and organizational interests of its members. NPA publishes the biweekly *Hotline; Success in Newsletter Publishing, a Practical Guide,* and statistical studies of the newsletter industry. Seminars and workshops on topics pertinent to the newsletter industry are held periodically. A publications list is available.

Labels

Almost every organization uses labels of one kind or another. Buy labels that fit your software templates. Label measurements must match your label template exactly, and for laser printers, there must be no gaps that expose the backing. Be sure to buy genuine laser labels.

Avery Dennison
P O Box 60786
Pasadena, CA 91116-6786
Consumer Service Center: 1-800-462-8379

Avery offers full sheet and single-column white and clear address labels, as well as a variety of other products for use with desktop printers. You can print the labels using many popular word processing, spreadsheet and database programs, or you can use Avery's own software (Label Pro or MacLabel Pro).

MACO
225 Long Avenue
Hillside, NJ 07205
1-800-221-9983

MACO offers most of the popular labels in the same sizes as Avery, keyed to the Avery numbering system so you can use the templates in your word processor.

Preprinted Papers

Paper Direct Inc.
205 Chubb Avenue
Lyndhurst, NJ 07071
1-800-A-PAPERS

This mail order company was a pioneer in preprinted papers. The PaperDirect catalog offers a broad range of papers and imaginative software products you can use with your computer and printer to create full-color letterheads, brochures, business cards, complete presentation sets, certificates, mailing envelopes, labels and others.

Quill
100 Schelter Road
Lincolnshire, IL 60069-3621
1-800-789-5813

Quill is an office supply mail order company that has entered the
preprinted papers market with a line of bordered papers, "brochure-ready"
decorated paper, seals, stationery, envelopes, postcards and other products.
Quill claims to be the lowest cost supplier of preprinted papers.

Image Street
Moore Business Products & Services
Lake Forest, IL 60061
1-800-462-4378

A new entry in the preprinted papers market from a company that has been
making business forms for many years. Their specialty: "cohesively designed
complete promotional kits."

Periodicals

Technique
The How-to Guide to Successful Communications
Print Publishing Inc.
9 Park Street
Boston, MA 02108-4807
1-800-4-TECHIE

Focuses on the design of business communications.

Home Office Computing
Scholastic Inc.
411 Lafayette Street
New York, NY 10003
800-288-7812

A good resource for startup operations.

MAIL: The Journal of Communication Distribution
Excelsior Publications
One Milstone Road
Gold Key Box 2425
Milford, PA 18337-9607
717-686-2111

Slanted toward large organizations' mailing operations.

PC Novice
P.O. Box 85380
Lincoln, NE 68501-9807
402-479-2104

For the beginner.

Business Mail Services

Consulting

The United States Postal Service
Postal Business Centers

The USPS has established more than 95 Postal Business Centers all over the country. Each has a staff of experienced postal consultants. There is no charge for their helpful information. They also offer unique mailing aids, such as plastic templates for reply mail layouts.

Your local Postal Business Center is open from 8:30 a.m. to 5:00 p.m. every business day. Call your local post office to locate your Business Center.

Mailing Services

If you want to spend your time planning new campaigns, use a service bureau to handle the ones you've already thought out.

Sheltered Workshops

Clients stuff envelopes and stamp or meter them under close supervision. You can support a worthy cause at the same time you're getting your work done.

Neighborhood Print/Mail Shops

Many neighborhood print shops offer mailing services such as outputting your list to labels or envelopes.

DirectNET

In step with the 90s trend toward virtual everything, Pitney Bowes recently initiated a new full-service remote mailing operation that brings to small businesses the advantages of a big business mail center. DirectNET handles the whole job from merge to mailbox.

Here's how it works:

- Write, design and set up your mailing piece.

- Submit your order, the mailing piece and your list by modem.

- DirectNET prints it, addresses it and mails it.

You pay postage and a modest per-piece charge.

DirectNET Mailing Services
35 Waterview Drive
Shelton, CT 06484-8000
1-800-461-2853

Mail Order

Mailer's Software, Inc.
970 Calle Negocio
San Clemente, CA 92673-6201
1-800-800-MAIL

This unique mail order catalog offers software and other products designed for mailing, database marketing and telemarketing.

Postally Correct Miscellany

This section is a collection of Postally Correct facts that will help you plan your mailings and address them correctly.

ZIP Codes, Barcodes and FIMS

None of today's postal automation would be possible without the ZIP Code system and **POST**al **N**umeric **E**ncoding **T**echnique code, POSTNET—the foundation of USPS system.

The ZIP Code system

In 1963, the Postal Service took the first step beyond manual processing when it introduced the mechanized ZIP Code system. Nineteen years later, it replaced the original system with a new automated process that relies on the expanded ZIP+4 system. The system works in conjunction with POSTNET, a barcode system developed for the Postal Service.

The system is easy to understand if you keep in mind that ZIP Codes are printed in ordinary Arabic numbers and POSTNET codes are printed as bars.

ZIP Codes	*Delivery Points*
5-Digit ZIP Code Example: 12345	Geographic location (digits 1 to 3) in the U.S. and specific delivery post office (digits 4 and 5).

ZIP+4
    ZIP Code plus 4-digit sector number.
    Example: 12345-6789
	Delivery sector: several blocks, groups of streets, several office buildings or a small geographic area.

ZIP+4 (+ 2 barcode digits)
    ZIP+4 + two additional *barcode digits* representing the last 2 digits in the primary street address.
    Example:
    101 East Avenue
    12345-6789
	Automatically feeds to the station for the carrier who delivers this mail. Delivery segment: one floor of a building, one side of a street, specific departments in a company or a group of P.O. boxes.

ZIP+4 (+ 4 barcode digits)
    ZIP+4+2 plus two more *barcode digits* representing the 2-digit carrier code.
    Example:
    CAR RT XX
    address block
    101 East Avenue
    12345-6789
	Special list management software automatically ZIP-sorts down to the walk sequence level, the order in which the carrier delivers the mail.

Cracking the POSTNET Code

Although it takes sophisticated equipment to read it, POSTNET is a simple system as barcodes go. It's very easy to print compared to other more complex codes such as the "3 of 9," for example. POSTNET could be called 3 of 5 because three of the five bars in a POSTNET digit are short bars.

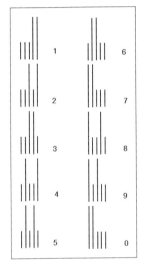

POSTNET Digits

Every POSTNET code starts and ends with a single tall bar called the frame bar, and just before the end frame bar, a whole five-bar digit called the correction bar. The correction bar is a value that brings the total of all the barcode digits to a number divisible by 10. If the number is already divisible by 10, the correction digit is a zero.

Here is an ordinary five-digit barcode complete with frame and correction bars.

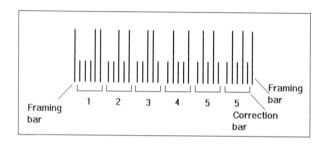

The five-digit code, 12345, adds up to 15; the correction digit is a 5, bringing the sum of the numbers to 20.

FIM A, B & C

The Facing Identification Mark (FIM) has a very important role on the reply device. Every piece of Business Reply Mail must have a FIM.

Remember the comment about getting your own mail back? If you send a postcard with the prospect's address on the front, and your address on the back, the FIM forces the automated equipment to read the correct side. If you do have to show your address, make sure it isn't OCR-readable. (Print in italic type or a light shade of ink.)

Facing Identification Marks are patterns of six tall black bars separated by thick or thin white bars. There are three FIM patterns. The type of reply mail determines which FIM to use.

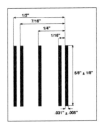

FIM A: Courtesy Reply Mail (prebarcoded) that's metered or stamped.

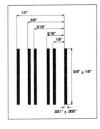

FIM B: Unbarcoded Business Reply Mail with no prepaid postage. This FIM is used by very large companies for centralized mass mailings where the reply will come back to regional offices. The replies carry the regional FIMs and barcodes.

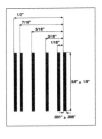

FIM C: Prebarcoded Business Reply Mail that bears a permit imprint. This mail is also prepaid but the originator only pays for it if it is returned.

Postal Discounts

Not every business is looking for discounts for their mailings. Sometimes the appearance of a hand-stamped First-Class letter outweighs the savings. Nevertheless, with new rulings coming out every year, it is more and more important to know where to find this information when you need it.

Minimum quantities required for discounts at press time range from 200 to 500 pieces depending on the service required. Discounts run from about 4 ½% to over 20% off full price.

> ***Memo to Mailers.*** *1) Mail must have a ZIP+4 Code on the label or envelope to qualify for any discount. 2) Check with your post office for current discount rates and classifications.*

Bulk mail can be metered or show a permit imprint. Some categories allow the use of stamps. See your post office for a complete list of requirements.

Here are the current bulk rate categories for First-Class Mail in ascending order of greater discount: Each class offers similar discounts.

- Nonsorted ZIP+4:* Must have ZIP+4, OCR-readable, machinable, barcode clear zone. The permit reads: FIRST CLASS U.S. POSTAGE PAID.

- Nonsorted ZIP+4 BARCODE: Must have ZIP+4, barcode, BCR-readable, machinable, barcode clear zone. The permit reads: FIRST CLASS U.S. POSTAGE PAID.

- Presorted:* Must sort 10 or more per 5-digit ZIP, 50 or more for 3-digit ZIP. The permit reads: PRESORTED FIRST CLASS U.S. POSTAGE PAID.

- 3/5 Digit Presorted ZIP+4: * Must have ZIP+4 on 85% of the mailing, OCR-readable, machinable, barcode clear zone. Must sort 10 or more for 5-digit ZIP; 50 or more for 3-digit ZIP. The permit reads: PRESORTED FIRST CLASS U.S. POSTAGE PAID.

---

* Stamps permitted.

- Presorted ZIP+4 Barcode (3-Digit): Must have ZIP+4 barcode on 85% of mailing, machinable, barcode clear zone. Must sort 50 or more for 3-digit ZIP. The permit reads: PRESORTED FIRST CLASS U.S. POSTAGE PAID.

- Presorted ZIP+4 Barcode (5-Digit): Must have ZIP+4 Barcode on 85% of mailing, machinable, barcode clear zone. Must sort 10 or more 5-digit ZIP. The permit reads: CARRIER ROUTE FIRST CLASS U.S. POSTAGE PAID.

Special Services

When mailing individual pieces, sometimes it's smart to use one or more of the USPS special services. Only five of them concern us here—Certificate of Mailing, Certified Mail, Registered Mail, Restricted Delivery and Return Receipt. Which do you use, when?

To prove you mailed something: Ask for a *Certificate of Mailing* when you mail it. Although this document offers an inexpensive way to prove a piece was accepted for mailing by the USPS, it doesn't prove it was delivered and it doesn't give you insurance coverage. For a fee at the time of mailing, you may receive a certificate of mailing for single pieces of First-Class and third- and fourth-class mail.

For proof of receipt: Use *Certified Mail* instead of Registered Mail when proof of mailing is the real concern and the piece has no cash or intrinsic value. Unlike Registered Mail, you don't have to take it to the post office to mail it. The record of delivery kept at your recipient's post office for two years will prove that your letter was delivered, and when. You don't get a delivery receipt with Certified Mail, but you can buy a return receipt separately. More expensive than a Certificate of Mailing, Certified Mail is available only for First-Class Mail. (For international mail, use Recorded Delivery.)

Express Mail guarantees overnight domestic delivery of your most urgent packages and letters, weekends and holidays included. Not surprisingly, it's the most expensive delivery service the USPS offers.

For valuable and important mail: Use *Registered Mail.* No other form of postal service can match it for providing peace of mind, plus evidence of mailing and optional proof of delivery. The most secure delivery for items sent by First-Class Mail or Priority Mail, Registered Mail receives special handling from the mailing point to the delivery office. There is a charge for Registered Mail and you can also buy insurance, a return receipt and restricted delivery.

Registered Mail does have some drawbacks. The extra security can delay the mail by an extra 24 to 48 hours. Also, you may decide the high cost isn't worth such an extreme level of security.

For extra security or privacy: Use *Restricted Delivery* which limits receipt of your piece to the addressee or someone authorized in writing to receive that person's mail. For a fee, you can add Restricted Delivery to Registered Mail, Certified Mail, COD mail and mail that is insured for more than $50.

For even greater peace of mind: Request a *Return Receipt* for a special mailing. A Return Receipt is your written proof of delivery; it shows when the piece was delivered and who received it.

The Postal Service has found that many mailers request return receipts out of habit rather than need. You can probably save money by taking a hard look at the value of this service before you buy it. You can buy a Return Receipt at the time you send your mail, only for mail sent by Express Mail or COD, mail that is insured for more than $50, and Registered or Certified Mail.

Standard Postal Abbreviations

The USPS has established standard abbreviations for elements of the outside address. Your mail will progress through the system faster if you use them.

Two-Letter State and Possession Abbreviations

Alabama	AL	Maryland	MD
Alaska	AK	Massachusetts	MA
Arizona	AZ	Michigan	MI
Arkansas	AR	Minnesota	MN
American Samoa	AS	Mississippi	MS
California	CA	Missouri	MO
Colorado	CO	Montana	MT
Connecticut	CT	Nebraska	NE
Delaware	DE	Nevada	NV
District of Columbia	DC	New Hampshire	NH
Federated States of Micronesia	FM	New Jersey	NJ
Florida	FL	New Mexico	NM
Georgia	GA	New York	NY
Guam	GU	North Carolina	NC
Hawaii	HI	North Dakota	ND
Idaho	ID	Northern Mariana Islands	MP
Illinois	IL	Ohio	OH
Indiana	IN	Oklahoma	OK
Iowa	IA	Oregon	OR
Kansas	KS	Palau	PW
Louisiana	LA	Texas	TX
Maine	ME	Utah	UT
Marshall Islands	MH	Vermont	VT

More Two-Letter State and Possession Abbreviations

Pennsylvania	PA	Virginia	VA
Puerto Rico	PR	Virgin Islands	VI
Rhode Island	RI	Washington	WA
South Carolina	SC	West Virginia	WV
South Dakota	SD	Wisconsin	WI
Tennessee	TN	Wyoming	WY

Abbreviations for Street Designators (Street Suffixes)

Alley	ALY	Center	CTR
Annex	ANX	Circle	CIR
Arcade	ARC	Cliffs	CLFS
Avenue	AVE	Club	CLB
Bayou	BYU	Corner	COR
Beach	BCH	Corners	CORS
Bend	BND	Course	CRSE
Bluff	BLF	Court	CT
Bottom	BTM	Courts	CTS
Boulevard	BLVD	Cove	CV
Branch	BR	Creek	CRK
Bridge	BRG	Crescent	CRES
Brook	BRK	Crossing	XING
Burg	BG	Dale	DL
Bypass	BYP	Dam	DM
Camp	CP	Divide	DV
Canyon	CYN	Drive	DR
Cape	CPE	Estates	EST
Causeway	CSWY	Expressway	EXPY

More Abbreviations for Street Designators (Street Suffixes)

Extension	EXT	Inlet	INLT
Fall	FALL	Island	IS
Falls	FLS	Islands	ISS
Ferry	FRY	Isle	ISLE
Field	FLD	Junction	JCT
Fields	FLDS	Key	KY
Flats	FLT	Knolls	KNLS
Ford	FRD	Lakes	LKS
Forest	FRST	Landing	LNDG
Forge	FRG	Lane	LN
Fork	FRK	Light	LGT
Forks	FRKS	Loaf	LF
Fort	FT	Locks	LCKS
Freeway	FWY	Lodge	LDG
Gardens	GDNS	Loop	LOOP
Gateway	GTWY	Mall	MALL
Glen	GLN	Manor	MNR
Green	GRN	Meadows	MDWS
Grove	GRV	Mill	ML
Harbor	HBR	Mills	MLS
Haven	HVN	Mission	MSN
Heights	HTS	Mount	MT
Highway	HWY	Mountain	MTN
Hill	HL	Neck	NCK
Hills	HLS	Orchard	ORCH
Hollow	HOLW	Oval	OVAL

More Abbreviations for Street Designators (Street Suffixes)

Park	PARK	Spring	SPG
Parkway	PKY	Springs	SPGS
Pass	PASS	Spur	SPUR
Path	PATH	Square	SQ
Pike	PIKE	Station	STA
Pines	PNES	Stravenue	STRA
Place	PL	Street	ST
Plain	PLN	Summit	SMT
Plains	PLNS	Terrace	TER
Plaza	PLZ	Trace	TRCE
Point	PT	Track	TRAK
Port	PRT	Trail	TRL
Prairie	PR	Trailer	TRLR
Radial	RADL	Tunnel	TUNL
Ranch	RNCH	Turnpike	TPKE
Rapids	RPDS	Union	UN
Rest	RST	Valley	VLY
Ridge	RDG	Viaduct	VIA
River	RIV	View	VW
Road	RD	Village	VLG
Row	ROW	Ville	VL
Run	RUN	Vista	VIS
Shoal	SHL	Walk	WALK
Shoals	SHLS	Way	WAY
Shore	SHR	Wells	WLS
Shores	SHRS		

Directional Abbreviations

North	N
East	E
South	S
West	W
Northeast	NE
Southeast	SE
Southwest	SW
Northwest	NW

Secondary Address Unit Indicators

Apartment	APT
Building	BLDG
Floor	FL
Room	RM
Department	DEPT

The *MAIL IT!* Library

The Library is in two parts: A listing of favorite books by experts in the design, production and delivery of market-driven, PC-generated mail, followed by some of the references used for this book.

Recommended Reading

_____. *The Chicago Manual of Style.* The University of Chicago Press, 1982

A definitive style manual. This updated 13th edition reflects the technological advances made in publishing procedures. Essential in any desktop marketing library.

_____. *GATF Glossary of Graphic Arts Terms*. Graphic Arts Technical Foundation, 1991

Updated annually by GATF, this is a useful glossary of terms specific to the graphic communications industries.

_____. *History of the United States Postal Service, 1775-1993*. U.S. Postal Service, September, 1993

_____. *How to Grow Your Business Using the Mail*. Pitney Bowes, Inc., 1992

A useful handbook on planning your mail marketing campaign.

_____. *The New York Times Manual of Style and Usage*. Revised and edited by Lewis Jordan, News Editor, New York Times, 1991

A desk book of guidelines used by the writers and editors of *The New York Times.*

_____. *Postal Addressing Standards,* Publication 28. United States Postal Service, 1992

An overview of postal addressing standards. A must for all business mailers who are looking for ways to reduce postal costs and improve deliverability.

_____. *Webster's Collegiate Thesaurus.* Merriam Webster, Inc., 1988

A well-respected edition of this standard, with more than 100,000 synonyms, antonyms, idiomatic phrases, related and contrasted words.

Arnold, Paul A., Christine C. Stern, Theresa Snider. *Postal Business Companion.* Braddock Communications, Inc. United States Postal Service, 1994

An informative paperback covering the services available at the USPS Postal Centers.

Book, Albert C. *Fundamentals of Copy and Layout.* NTC Business Books, 1984

A practical, comprehensive paperback that covers how to write and design effective, powerful advertising for all forms of media.

Bruno, Michael H., Editor. *Pocket Pal.* International Paper Company, 1992

Since the first edition in 1934, this "graphic arts production handbook" has been the dog-eared companion to countless beleaguered production managers.

Beach, Mark, Steve Shepro, Ken Russon. *Getting it Printed.* Coast to Coast Books, 1986

A production manager's right hand.

The Lunch Group and Guests. *Digital Deli.* Steve Ditlea, Editor. Workman Publishing, 1984

All the computer trivia you'll ever need to know in one volume. Delightful reading with wonderful insights by a variety of authors.

Nash, Edward L., Editor in Chief. *The Direct Marketing Handbook.* McGraw Hill, 1992

An encyclopedic desktop reference. Insights into every conceivable facet of direct marketing. Over 40 acknowledged experts share their wisdom and advice.

Skillin, Marjorie E., Robert M. Gay et al. *Words into Type, Third Edition.* Prentice Hall, 1974

An authoritative aid for writers, copyeditors and production managers.

Strunk, William, E.B. White. *The Elements of Style, Third Edition.* Macmillian Publishing Co., Inc., 1979

This venerable treasure is the essential aid to every writer for grammar, syntax and common sense.

Zinsser, William Knowlton. *On Writing Well: An informal guide to writing, 4th edition.* HarperPerennial, 1990

The enemy of the stuffed shirt shares his wisdom.

Zinsser, William Knowlton. *Writing with a Word Processor.* Harper & Row, 1983

Wise and funny observations on getting started with a word processor.

Selected Bibliography

_____.Archives, Pitney Bowes, Inc.

A matchless collection of history, humor and evolutionary machinery for the future Pitney Bowes Museum.

_____.Archives, Xerox Corporation.

An interesting history of changing technology from 1905 to today. The Xerox Museum in Rochester, New York, tells the story with representative equipment.[1]

_____. *Communicating Caterpillar: One Voice.* Caterpillar Inc.

An excellent, reasoned approach to corporate design.

_____. *Domestic Mail Manual 47.* United States Postal Service, 1994

An 882-page tome, the DMM is the USPS official word on how to speed your domestic mail on its way.

_____. *Standards & Guidelines.* GE Identity Program CD-ROM, 1995

A comprehensive corporate identity program and a wonderful way to look at a very large set of books.

_____. *Corporate Identity Control Manual.* Pitney Bowes, Inc.

_____. *mail flow planning system.* United States Postal Service, 1994

An interactive DOS program that gives an in-depth understanding of how postal automation technology can result in faster mail processing and substantial savings.

---

1 The Xerox Museum, 2619 West Henrietta Road, Rochester, NY 14623.
  Call 716-427-4207 for hours and tour information.

_____. *Wharton Study on Graphics and Presentations.* Wharton Center for Applied Research, University of Pennsylvania, 1985

_____. *1995 Xerox Fact Book.* Xerox Corporation, 1995

DeLoca, Cornelius E. and Samuel Jay Karlow. *The Romance Division...A Different Side of IBM.* D & K Book Company, Inc., 1991[2]

The history, strategies and key people involved in the Electric Typewriter Division and its successor, the Office Products Division of IBM—the role they played in the creation of today's office systems and automation industry.

Document Design: A Review of the Relevant Research. Daniel B. Felker, Editor. American Institutes for Research, 1980

A review on how to make forms, regulations, brochures and other written materials easier for people to read, understand and use.

Felker, Daniel B., F. Pickering, V.R. Charrow, V.M. Holland, and J.C. Redish. *Guidelines for Document Designers.* American Institutes for Research, 1981

The presentation of twenty-five principles that can make the documents you write easier to read and understand.

Felker, Daniel B., J.C. Redish, and J. Peterson. *Designing Usable Texts.* Chapter 3, Academic Press, Inc., 1985

This chapter covers the training of authors who write material of practical value to the real world. It is the result of research done on how to write usable and understandable documents.

2 Supplemented by interviews with other IBM veterans

Harmon, Craig K., and Russ Adams. *Reading Between the Lines.* North American Technology, Inc., 1985

An introduction to barcode technology.

Lewis, Elaine, David Sykes, and Peter H. Lemieux. *Empirical Comparison of the Effectiveness of Typeset, Typewritten and Dot Matrix Business Documents.* The Project for Interdisciplinary Research in Information, School and Public Communications, Boston University, 1984[3]

Tufte, Edward R. *The Visual Display of Quantitative Information.* Graphics Press, 1992

A landmark book on the presentation of statistical graphics; on communicating information through the simultaneous presentation of words, numbers and pictures.

Solomon, Martin. *The Art of Typography.* Watson-Guptill Publications, 1986

An introduction to understanding contemporary type design through classic typography.

Taintor, Sarah Augusta. *The Secretary's Handbook,* 10th Edition. Revision by Margaret D. Shertzer. Macmillan, 1988

Yeck, John D. "Lessons from the Rear View Mirror."

An address to the Business to Business Forum, 1983

3 Commissioned by Compugraphics Corporation

Glossary

Aspect Ratio:

> Used to determine if mail is machinable. Divide the length (the dimension parallel to the lines of the delivery address) of the mail piece by its height. If the aspect ratio falls between 1.3 and 2.5, your mail is machinable.

Barcode:

> Series of vertical full and half bars. Enables a barcode sorter to identify the destination ZIP Code of the mailpiece and sort it accurately.

Barcode Digit:

> See Code Character.

Barcode Clear Zone:

> Area at the lower right corner of envelope that must be free of extraneous printing so the OCR can read or print a barcode.

Barcode Sorter (BCS):

> Mail processing machine that reads barcodes on mail and automatically sorts the pieces.

Baseline:

> The imaginary line on which a printed character rests. Ascending and descending strokes (d or y, for example) extend above and below the baseline.

Basis Weight:

Weight in pounds of 500 sheets of paper (a ream) of the basic precut size of a particular sheet. The minimum basis weight for machinability of envelopes is 16 pounds.

Bit:

Contraction of "binary digit"—the basic unit of information used in computers. A bit can have only one of two values, zero or one. In POSTNET barcodes, full bars represent a one bit; half bars, a zero bit.

Boilerplate:

Standard paragraphs that can be assembled in a variety of combinations to form semi-personalized letters.

Bounceback:

A reply device. An envelope or card preprinted to be returned to the originator; may or may not be postage paid.

Bulk Mail Center (BMC):

Mechanized mail processing plant which primarily handles bulk second-, third- and fourth-class mail.

Business Reply Mail (BRM):

A service by which you can receive First-Class Mail back from customers, paying postage only on the mail actually returned to you.

Byte:

Eight bits of data, roughly equivalent to one character.

Carrier Route Code:
> A code assigned to an individual mail carrier. Prebarcoded mail that includes this information can be sorted down to the carrier's order of delivery ("walk sequence").

CASS:
> Coding Accuracy Support System. This U.S. Postal Service program certifies certain software vendors and other information services suppliers to provide official ZIP+4 and address correction services to the public. To be eligible for the best automation discounts, verify and correct your mailing list using CASS-certified software.

CD, CD-ROM:
> (Compact Disc, Compact-Disc Read-Only Memory) a storage medium that holds many times the capacity of a floppy disk. Strictly speaking, CDs refer to audio discs; CD-ROMs to digital storage for computers.

Cheshire Labels:
> Mailing labels on specially prepared paper: rolls, fan-fold or accordion-fold continuous form papers used to reproduce names and addresses to be mechanically affixed one at a time to a mailing piece. They are generally printed on standard computer paper.

Code Character:
> In the POSTNET barcode, a combination of two full bars and three half bars representing a specific digit from 0 to 9.

Color Break:
> On a mechanical tissue overlay, an indication of a change of color.

Color Matching System:

> As used in printing, predefined colors with specific ingredients and percentages for the purpose of assuring true color printing.

Co-op Mailing:

> Pool your mail with another organization and share the cost.

Correction Character:

> In the POSTNET barcode, a five-bar symbol placed immediately before the right frame bar in all POSTNET barcodes. The correction character stands for a digit which, when added to the other digits in the ZIP Code, produces a total that is a multiple of 10.

Courtesy Reply Mail:

> Self-addressed, prebarcoded mail to be returned to the originator. Courtesy reply mail does not carry prepaid postage.

Crop:

> Cut or mask part of a picture without distorting it.

Database:

> Collection of information stored in a computer file. A common example is a computerized mailing list.

Default:

> A standard value preset by a computer system or application. Example: Lines per page = 66.

Delivery Point Barcode (DPBC):

    ZIP+4 barcode containing two additional digits representing the last two digits in the street address, plus two more barcode digits representing the mail carrier's code. DPBC allows mail sorting in the order it is delivered on a carrier route.

Demographics:

    Characteristics of a population defined by age, sex, race, income or other social or economic criteria.

Desktop Publishing:

    The use of special page composition software to prepare complex textual and graphical material for printing.

Direct Marketing:

    Sales promotion technique that uses the mail to generate leads or orders direct from the individual. Other forms are telemarketing and door-to-door selling.

Directional:

    One of eight geographic elements of an address indicating a specific area, such as Pacific Boulevard NW.

Extension:

    On a DOS or Windows system, the part of a filename after the period that indicates the filetype (FILENAME.DOC or FILENAME.DBF, for example). .DOC is a typical word processing extension and .DBF is a typical database extension.

Faced Mail:

>   Mail arranged with the address/postage side of each piece facing the same way.

Facer-Canceler:

>   Automated machine that orients mail correctly for canceling postage. It separates machine-addressed letters for processing on optical character readers (which see). The machine also reads Facing Identification Marks (FIM) on business reply and courtesy reply mail and separates it for further automated processing.

Facing Identification Mark (FIM):

>   Special barcode that enables automated mail processing equipment to identify and separate business reply and courtesy reply mail from other mail. The FIM identifies the delivery address side of a mailpiece.

Flats:

>   Mail exceeding at least one of the dimensions for letter-sized mail, but none of the maximum dimensions for flat-size mail.

Folio, Drop Folio:

>   Page numbers that appear in margin text. Drop folios are page numbers in footers.

Font:

>   The entire collection of characters, including punctuation and special symbols of one point size in a given typeface.

FPO:

>   For Position Only. Indicates a placeholder on a mockup or mechanical.

Frame Bar:

>   A full or tall bar that begins and ends each POSTNET barcode. Gives the barcode sorter a reference point to start and stop reading the barcode.

Franked Mail:

>   (Also called free-franked mail.) Mail that has privileged status and travels through the system without charge. Government officials use franked mail.

Geographic Information System (GIS):

>   A software program that presents statistical data in reference to a map, among other views.

Gothic:

>   A plain typeface; no curlicues. Sans serif type.

Graphical User Interface (GUI):

>   A computer screen layout and mouse-driven command system that uses icons, menus and dialog boxes to communicate with the user.

Hard Copy:

>   Printout of information stored on a computer disk.

Hard Disk:

>   An internal storage device with much greater storage capacity than a floppy disk. Also called the hard drive.

Imposition:

>   The arrangement of page sets for a dummy or mechanical to ensure they will be printed in the correct sequence for folding and binding.

Indicia:
> Preprinted marking of each piece of a bulk mailing showing that the sender has prepaid the postage (called Permit Imprint in this book).

Integral Proof:
> A single proof page showing the separate colors as they will be printed together.

Johnson Box:
> For promotional mail, a section of copy enclosed with asterisks, bullets or some other border.

Leading:
> Line spacing. Word processors and page composition programs can fine-tune line spacing by fractions of inches.

Logo, Logotype:
> A statement or symbol identifying an organization.

Machinable:
> Refers to mail of the right size, weight and material to move at high speed through the automated mail processing system.

Mailing Statements:
> Forms required by the Postal Service as verification for a bulk mailing.

Masthead:
> The area in a periodical devoted to publisher's information.

Mechanical:
> Complete text and graphics material laid out with great precision on a board to be filmed for printing.

Merge/Purge:
> Process of combining two or more mailing lists and deleting duplicate names and addresses.

National Change of Address System (NCOA):
> Comprehensive Postal Service program that gives you current change of address information to help reduce undeliverable mail. Under license from the USPS, private businesses maintain address lists on magnetic tape or diskette. For a small fee, you can match your lists against the NCOA lists to identify and correct addressing errors before you mail.

Nixie Elimination Service:
> A refinement of the National Change of Address System that warns you that a customer might have moved. A series of footnotes allow you to assess how similar the match is, then decide whether or not to mail to the name and address in question.

OCR-Readable:
> Mail with a machine-printed address or postal barcode that can be read by an optical scanner.

OCR Read Area:
> The part of an envelope or card that must be kept clear of print other than an address.

One-Off:
> A letter, envelope or label produced one at a time.

Optical Character Reader (OCR):
Computerized mail processing machine that scans addresses on mail and prints the corresponding barcode on the piece.

Orphan:
The last line of a paragraph left alone at the top of a column or page.

Outer:
A term coined to mean the outside envelope of a direct marketing piece.

Overlay Proof:
Separate acetate sheets showing each color to be printed in register. Looked at from the top, all colors can be seen at once.

Permit Imprint:
(Indicia) A marking that substitutes for a stamp on each piece of a bulk mailing. Printed directly on the mailpiece, the imprint shows your permit number, which identifies your account. You pay postage through this account.

Pica:
A printer's measure equal to about one-sixth of an inch; 12 *points* (which see).

Pitch:
The number of characters of type per inch; 12-pitch type prints twelve characters to one horizontal inch.

Platform:
A particular type of computer hardware or operating system.

Point:

In typography, a printer's measure the equivalent of $1/72$ of an inch. Twelve-point type is $1/6$ of an inch high.

Postage Meter:

Machine that imprints prepaid postage on mailpieces in a special fluorescent ink.

POSTNET:

Acronym (POSTal Numeric Encoding Technique) for the USPS barcode that automates ZIP Code information.

Precanceled Stamps:

A postal option available only to bulk mailers. To use precanceled stamps, you need a permit filed at the post office where you will be depositing your mail. There's no charge for the permit.

Prebarcoding:

Using any of various software packages with your PC, you can print POSTNET barcodes on your outgoing mail before delivering it to the Postal Service, earning a discount.

Presort:

Postal program that offers discounts for separating your First-Class Mail by ZIP Code before mailing. This saves the Postal Service handling and processing time, and improves delivery accuracy. You can presort 10 or more pieces to the same carrier route for further savings.

Press Check:

Sampling the output of the printing press at the printing plant.

Press Sheet:

A sample pulled from a press run to check color registration, quality and so on.

Proportional Spacing:

Arrangement of characters in a line so each occupies a space proportional to its width. Contrast fixed spacing, where every character occupies the same amount of space regardless of its width.

Propositional Density:

Writing so packed with content it's hard to digest.

Registration:

The precise alignment of color and other printing details on the press sheet. Registration marks printed outside the readable area are used to line up the elements.

Remote Barcoding System (RBCS):

The USPS attempts to barcode all mail, even handwritten pieces and other mail the OCR can't read. That mail is sent to the RBCS where an image of the front of the envelope is displayed on a computer screen. An operator corrects the bad information and the RBCS recycles the letter through the system.

Resolution:

In desktop publishing, the dots-per-inch (DPI) value rendered by the printer or the pixels per inch (PPI) value rendered by a scanner.

River:

A distracting streak of contiguous white space running down a page through the text.

Roman:

A typeface with "hooks" on the elements. Serif type.

Rules:

A graphic arts term for lines.

Sans Serif:

A typeface without finishing strokes. Also called gothic.

Sectional Center Facility (SCF):

Mail processing unit serving a specific geographic area as determined by the first three digits of the ZIP Code.

Self-Mailer:

Any form of mail not sent in an envelope, sleeve, bag or box. Postage is affixed directly to the piece. Postcards, booklets, brochures and flyers are commonly sent as self-mailers.

Serif:

Typeface having fine lines that finish off the main letter strokes, as at the top and bottom of *M* or the cross stroke of *T*. See also sans serif.

Sorting:

Process of arranging pieces in a bulk mailing in order of ZIP Code.

Teaser:

A direct mail convention: envelope copy designed to get the recipient curious or interested enough to look inside.

Thumbnail Sketch:

A rough drawing of a concept or design.

Thumbnails:

Sheets of miniature pages showing the pagination and imposition of a work. Some page composition programs can generate thumbnails.

Typeface:

A complete set of characters of a given style in a range of sizes. Goudy Oldstyle is a typeface.

Type Family:

The broad term that includes all the typefaces and typestyles in a related group. A partial listing of the Goudy family includes Goudy Oldstyle, Goudy Bold Italic, Goudy Cursive, Goudy Handtooled and so on.

Typestyle:

One of the type attributes. Bold and Italic are typestyles.

Volatile Memory:

Temporary or working memory used by the computer to make your file available for changes.

White Space:

Background for the information on a page. Used as a design element, analogous to the painter's trick of visualizing empty spaces as opposed to solids.

Widow:

>A single line at the beginning of a paragraph left stranded at the bottom of a column or page.

Word Processing:

>Word processing is the computerized creation of text documents.

Word Wrap:

>The cornerstone of word processing. You type through the end of the line; the system automatically throws excess text to the next line. You press RETURN only for short lines or paragraphs.

WP:

>Acronym for word processing.

WYSIWYG:

>"What You See Is What You Get." Term for an image on a computer screen that closely approximates the way the printed output will appear.

ZIP+4 Code:

>Nine-digit code that enables automated equipment to pinpoint a mailpiece's destination.

Index

Index

A

B

Q

R

Picture Credits

Evolution of a Corporate Identity • 10

Xerox Corporation • 10

General Electric Company • 12

General Electric Company • 13

Caterpillar Inc. • 14

Microsoft Corporation • 20

Microsoft Corporation • 23

Microsoft Corporation • 25

Microsoft Corporation • 27

Microsoft Corporation • 29

Microsoft Corporation • 30

Microsoft Corporation • 32

General Electric Company • 51

Pitney Bowes, Inc. • 53

Caterpillar Inc. • 62

Pitney Bowes, Inc. • 67

SNET • 68

Pitney Bowes, Inc. • 72

Pitney Bowes, Inc. • 74

SNET • 75

Pitney Bowes, Inc. • 77

Paper Direct, Inc. • 80

SNET • 81

U.S. Postal Service • 83

Adobe Systems Corporation • 86

Microsoft Corporation • 97

Claris Corporation • 108

U.S. Postal Service • 149

U.S. Postal Service • 160

Co-Star Corporation • 174

Co-Star Corporation • 175

Pitney Bowes, Inc. • 176

Pitney Bowes, Inc. • 177

Pitney Bowes, Inc. • 178

Pitney Bowes, Inc. • 179

Strategic Mapping, Inc. • 181

U.S. Postal Service • 197

More Resources

Name: Telephone: FAX:

More Resources

Name: Telephone: FAX:

Notes

Notes

Notes

Notes